COLOR MONTAGE

A sampler of the material that is presented in this book

Centerbrook Architects

Steve Badanes

Mick Hales

Mick Hales

Cervin Robinson

Mark Citret

Dan Cornish

Al DeVido

Al DeVido

Steve Trout

Paul Ferrino

Michael Graves

THE SMALL HOUSE
An Artful Guide to Affordable Residential Design

THE SMALL HOUSE
An Artful Guide to Affordable Residential Design

Duo Dickinson

McGraw-Hill Book Company

New York   St. Louis   San Francisco   Auckland   Bogotá   Hamburg   Johannesburg
London   Madrid   Mexico   Montreal   New Delhi   Panama   Paris
São Paulo   Singapore   Sydney   Tokyo   Toronto

THE McGRAW-HILL BUILDING TYPES SERIES

Wells / Gentle Architecture (1981)

Watson & Labs / Climatic Design (1982)

White / Bookstore Planning and Design (1982)

Crowley and Zimmerman / Practical Passive Solar Design: A Guide to Homebuilding and Land Development (1983)

Redstone / Masonry in Architecture (1983)

Dickinson / Adding On: An Artful Guide to Affordable Residential Additions (1985)

Dibner & Dibner-Dunlap / Building Additions Design (1985)

Barr & Broudy / Designing to Sell: The Art of Retail Store Planning and Design (1986)

Bednar / The New Atrium (1986)

Dickinson / The Small House: An Artful Guide to Affordable Residential Design (1986)

Talcott, Hepler, and Wallach / The Home Planners' Guide to Residential Design (1986)

Wakabayashi / Earthquake-Resistant Building Design (1986)

Taranath / Structural Analysis and Design of Tall Buildings (1988)

Library of Congress Cataloging-in-Publication Data

Dickinson, Duo.
  The small house.

  Includes index.
  1. Small houses—United States—Designs and plans.
2. Architect-designed houses—United States—Designs
and plans. I. Title.
NA7205.D55 1986   728.3′7   85-23963
ISBN 0-07-016818-0

1234567890   HAL/HAL   8932109876

ISBN 0-07-016818-0

The editors for this book were Joan Zseleczky and Barbara B. Toniolo, the designers were Mark E. Safran and Duo Dickinson, and the production supervisor was Thomas G. Kowalczyk. It was set in ITC Garamond Light by University Graphics, Inc.

Printed and bound by Halliday Lithograph

Dedicated to the Families
Dickinson, Morison, and Clarkson

Contents

Foreword

The small house looms very large in the landscape of our architectural history. Firmly embedded in our consciousness is the American log cabin in the big woods, the little frame house out there on the prairie, the miner's shack in the Rockies, the roadside bungalow, as well as the teepee and the igloo. Our childhood pillow houses and treehouses form a part of this collective small-house heritage.

Somehow, in recent history the small house has been relegated to the past, when life was simpler and before the family room, the rumpus room, the den, or the three-car garage had been conceived as necessary embellishments to the American home. The little house had become a sort of nostalgic image of the storybook—brimming to the full with virtue, but no longer attainable. Now, however, with the drastic rise in conventional fuel costs, the small house has made a comeback—shorn of those encumbrances, stripped down and basic. Small-house design has become a noticed part of the architect's repertoire.

Actually, I have fantasized all my life about designing vast castles with endless twisting corridors, layers of labyrinthine spaces wrapping around distant interiors which open up deep inside, illuminated by mysterious sources of light. Always lurking in the back of my mind is the Victorian house of my grandparents. In this house one could take the most incredible journey—starting in the pitch-dark cellar full of piles of coal, storerooms of unidentifiable objects, and a demonic glowing furnace, then wandering up through the main floors of light-filled bays with leaded windows, glowing amber woodwork, big dusky rooms with flowered wallpaper and solid fireplaces with clocks and trinkets on their mantles, expansive stairs, foyers, halls, and finally through a tiny angled door and up a narrow, winding, creaky stair with walls of dark beaded board to the attic, which, closed and stuffy, was full of musty smells, relics, and memories of ancestors.

However, in my own career as an architect I have mostly been asked to design the most humble of houses—impoverished descendants of the house of my memory. Yet I find the excitement of designing such a house is in part commensurate with how much of the mysterious, endless qualities of the original Victorian house can be worked into the confines of the small-house shell. Some of the success of the small house is based on how well it succeeds in feeling like a big house.

From the outside also it can be the little house playing at being a big house that is intriguing. The small but grand one-and-one-half-story Greek Revival houses do this very successfully by scaling up their trim work. The wide skirt board, the corner trim, and frieze board wrapping the facade compactly together, the doors and windows anchored into the facade by their generous wide casings, all this contrasts with the background of tiny clapboards, which, with their shadow lines, give a marvelous depth and solidity to the walls. They are solid, proud little buildings which inhabit the landscape with confidence.

But then too, there is something really wonderful about the very fact of smallness of the small house. The little house sitting out there alone on the landscape is one of the most moving images architecture has to offer. At night there is the little, taut, full object which glows warmly, light spilling out the windows, keeping the large dark landscape at bay.

The small house is most related to the concept of building as basic shelter from the elements. It is the safe space of the womb—familiar, protecting, and cozy. In the most direct sense, the small house becomes an extension of our bodies, its wall an outer layer of our skin which mediates between us and the less certain world outside. There is the overwhelming and satisfying sensation of being contained in the body of a small building confronting a larger space of landscape. That sensation goes back to childhood, when on rainy days we made houses of blankets draped over overturned chairs and tables, with pillows inside, cozily contained while looking out into the larger domain of the living room, which from that vantage point, seemed accessible as a friendly habitable extension of our private hidden space. It is also the experience of the tree house—hidden entirely from the outside world, but from within, the outside world accessible through gaps in the screen of leaves.

I like small-house clients. Often in my experience they have been semi-broke (thus bringing them close to the condition of the typical small-house architect), but at the same time they are very loyal to a project and they do pay up eventually even—if out of necessity—it's years later. Although they may have a strong and clear idea of how they want to live (the most fun ones do), they seem to have fewer preconceptions of how things should look than their more affluent counterparts. Perhaps they are just grateful to find someone who is willing to put an inexpensive roof over their heads. But one of the most rewarding aspects of small-house design for the architect can be the direct leap from the "napkin sketch" to the built work. Small houses more often embody the "idea" of the original rush of inspiration than do larger houses which can run amok by getting worked and reworked, sometimes to death, often as a result of endless changes demanded by the client who wields more money.

The best houses in this book investigate the nature of a small house without falling into the easy pitfall of becoming too cute, imitative, or quaint. The image of the archetypal small house is there, but also they are works of architecture dealing with particular issues of our time. Some have that wonderful aspect of being extremely humble in actual size but at the same time incredibly large, generous, and grand in spirit.

TURNER BROOKS

Preface

This book is not intended to be a scholarly work. Rather it is an attempt to provide a perspective on the state of a part of the science and art called architecture. The part to be examined and displayed is the small house, as designed by architects in the United States.

This book, while nonacademic, is not without bias. The architect-designed small house has often been a trifling display of aesthetic wit or an experimental prototype of implemented theory—often with dubious human utility or financial feasibility. Believing that the small house can be much more, I have written this book and I have chosen projects to inspire and delight both architect and home owner.

Submissions were solicited from publicly acclaimed architects, American Institute of Architects (A.I.A.) chapters, universities, and those personally referred to me.

Rather than simply select a hodgepodge of diverse, idiosyncratic works linked only by size, I have focused the presentation in this book on those works that embody a spirit rooted in the sense of "firmness, commodity, and delight" that transcends affected style and the cheap thrill. The result is a distillation of the work that represents the future of this building type.

* * *

At this time I'd like to thank Barbara Toniolo, Mark Safran, Edward Burke, and Susan Killikelly for their diligence in bringing this book into reality. My most thanks are to Joan Zseleczky for getting the ball rolling in the first place. Lastly, my deepest thanks to my wife Liz, without whom none of this would have been possible.

DUO DICKINSON

Introduction

I. EXISTING PERCEPTIONS

The small house is perceived in two contradictory ways in twentieth-century America. One perception is of projects designed by nonarchitects, the second is of small houses designed by professionals.

The first perception is of Levittown, of "ticky-tacky" little boxes, redundant, crowded together, and nestled to their streets, conveying a hopelessly thoughtless response to the need for cheap accommodation. These small houses were the logical elevation for families leaving the tenements of an immigrant generation. The desire to own four walls and a roof over their heads was great enough to allow forbearance of physical limitations.

This "half-a-loaf" philosophy can be seen today in the proliferation of nouvelle tenements otherwise known as condominiums.

The second perception is a contemporary one, though it has its roots in the beginnings of the Modern Movement, early in the twentieth century.

When a revolution sweeps a country, its leaders tend to be young. In aesthetic terms, a new vision can be expressed two-dimensionally, on canvas, paper, or board, with very limited monetary resources. In poetry, literature, or music, the financial investment is minimal. Sculpture requires more space, material, and, of course, cash.

All of these areas of artistic expression facilitate the creativity of impoverished young revolutionary aesthetes with relatively little patronage. But the world of architecture is different. There, tens of thousands of dollars are needed to implement even a small renovation. Obviously the high stakes of architectural patronage make experience more valuable than juvenile brilliance.

How then can young architects express themselves? Small houses by definition cost less than large houses. Architects tend to design for their contemporaries, hence Young Turk architects tend to design for other Young Turks—who have young bank accounts.

These economic realities affect the public perception of architect-designed small houses. The small houses receiving attention for their merit have generally been done by youthful missionaries with severely personal visions. Born of a lack of knowledge and a wealth of chutzpah, these houses reflect an explosion of repressed visions. Given the paucity of available paths for built expression, these small-house designers have often created manic frenzies of excruciatingly overwrought massing and detail, or constructions of such poetic distillation that they verge on functionless sculpture.

Time and experience bring more avenues for the designer to discover subtlety without losing the creative spark, or so one hopes. But in the wake of an architect's professional progression can lie several embarrassing failures in the form of small houses.

So, whether "crazy young architects" design homes with the appeal of lunar landers or anonymous builders replicate acres of congested boxes, the small house has a negative image in the minds of many.

It is hoped that this book will reveal an aspect of professionally designed smaller homes that will surprise and delight the reader. The projects displayed were chosen to convey a growing sense that the smaller home is no longer a stopgap solution or an architect's cruel joke. Because of demographic, geographic, and economic realities, the architect-designed small house is rapidly becoming the only uncompromising solution to the coming crisis in housing as the baby boom babies have babies.

II. THE NEED

A generation of Americans born after World War II and before 1960 has reached unprecedented affluence and social maneuverability at a tender age. With so much emphasis on career and personal control, the sizes of families have consistently shrunk over the last 2 decades until recent years, when the pent-up nesting desire has created a modest re-booming of families.

With divorce creating so many smaller family units, with extended life spans and non-nuclear families creating so many independent elderly, with childless "coupledom" now commonplace, and with the growing acceptance of single and gay lifestyles, our accommodations can and will "shrink to fit."

The "training wheels" for baby boomer home ownership might well be the now-conventional condominium. Condominium projects often have shared site services and structure and high population densities. They represent a new form of affluent ghetto, and the socioeconmic group typically accommodated is the smaller, more-affluent baby boom family.

So far, the home owners of today have evidenced the desire for quality over quantity in every personal possession save their homes. They choose automobiles that are smaller and better-designed and detailed than are their "full-size" counterparts. This generation buys clothes with designer labels and quality craftsmanship and materials, thereby decongesting their closets, as fewer, more-expensive, classically designed clothes supplant trendy impulse purchases. So it is with home furnishings: people are collecting their prized furniture and accoutrements over time versus buying a collected set of cheaper merchandise.

In light of this growing desire for quality over quantity and the reduced need for space brought about by many of the households seeking accommodation, what is needed now is a reexamination of traditional assumptions about what makes a home desirable. The unprecedented increased cost of financing and the ever-worsening scarcity of available building sites have pressurized the housing market to the point where there is more frustration than accommodation. This book presents an answer to the question of housing in an era of reduced spatial need and growing costs.

Multiple-family housing, whether in the form of urban co-ops, suburban condominiums, or rural cluster housing, does not serve well the simple human need for personal possession of home and environment. Forbearance of inadequacy can be justified when economics dictate, but the same financial plateau that accommodates the luxury of having a baby creates the need for ownership of more than just one's particular slot of space.

If the condominium is merely a Band-Aid solution, then what is the natural answer for a generation that has grown to value quality and has put new emphasis on pride in ownership? I advocate the freestanding, custom-designed home as the essential desire of all those forced into the condominium compromise. Since time tends to increase resources, I believe that the next generation of home owners will opt to exchange a communal parking lot for a picket fence. The viability of the single-family dwelling will be renewed via the simple cost-saving feature of making the house smaller.

In this book, I advocate architect-designed small houses as the best solution for a growing number of potential home owners. If you simply take a standard plan and erase the den and a bedroom, then set the photocopy machine to reduce by 15 percent, the results will be similar to the constrictive tract houses that are untenable as places in which to live in the 1980s. It is only by using knowledgeable architects that people can make sense of their homes in a world of shrinking expectations.

III. THE ROLE OF THE ARCHITECT

As stated, architects have created an image of unrestrained ego and thoughtless budget-busting. Unfortunately this image has been correct all too often.

Architectural students see Frank Lloyd Wright's Usonion houses, Le Corbusier's Villa Savoye, Mies van der Rohe's Farnsworth House, Philip Johnson's Glass House, or H. H. Richardson's Glessner House, and they are exposed to genius adapting to restrictive programs, sites, and budgets. They also see distilled aesthetic theory that is very compelling as a slide lecture or illustration in a book, but too often designed in an era when a polemic was more important than a conscience.

Leaving school, the architectural novitiate finds a job detailing or drafting someone else's designs, and daydreams of slides and heroes. When the opportunity presents itself, the protoarchitect unleashes his or her full aesthetic fury, and the results are often absurd enough to remain unbuilt.

It is the paradox of architecture that to gain competence you must have experience and that to get experience you must display competence. And then, once experience is gained, the profit motive tends to grow, leaving the small project, be it house or addition or renovation, in the realm of undesirable opportunity for some architects.

Why will the new generation of exurban condo expatriates use architects, given their track record for small houses?

In short, because they have no choice.

Small houses should not appear small or feel small. The only way to prevent a misfit or a binding abode is to maximize the efficiency of the house's working parts to liberate the house's living parts. The only way to counteract diminutive scale and potential aesthetic insignificance in a small house is to play with the scales available and reinforce a singular identity.

Can this be done by wishing? Obviously not. Can a person untrained or inexperienced combine spatial and formal delight with functional and structural efficiency? It would seem highly unlikely.

When these simple desires are combined with a great desire for energy efficiency, the prospects for high-quality nonprofessional design dim considerably. And when the oddball nature of most affordable sites (back lots, subdivisions, sites with poor access, etc.) is confronted, the need for an architect versed in small-house design is undeniable.

And yet, the vast majority of homes built in America today are not designed by licensed architects. So why should a small house be different?

Because it is small.

Not unlike a government that throws money at problems to solve them, those who make houses in America, architects or not, have traditionally thrown space at tricky problems. Architects have often used space as a design element, creating an enclosed environment on a scale with exterior space to enhance some aspect of their designs. But when a house is small by choice as well as necessity, space must be held to be sacred.

It is not only simple economics that imposes such limitations on home owners and designers. Every project has a budget. Money can be spent to create space and/or to create inspiring detail, use quality materials, or facilitate long-term economies of low-maintenance, energy-efficient design. The less space built, the greater the opportunity to invest time and money in those aspects of a building that provide the essential pride in ownership that motivates the home owner to build in the first place.

Obviously an architect, with professional perspective and creative insight, can help create a thoroughly efficient, aesthetically intriguing home. But without the client's direct and abiding input, the building will most assuredly fail in its most rudimentary purpose: to house people in a manner which best suits their needs.

The intimacy of mutual utility between the occupant and the designer of a new house is in direct proportion to the diminution of the building's size. Assumptions by the designer can be absurd when there is a lack of spatial lubricant for unplanned idiosyncratic behavior. A small house is very unforgiving of miscalculated priorities or neglected requirements.

The potential for architects is that while solving intimate problems they can convey essential aesthetic truths. The small house is not unlike a haiku poem. When conceived in thought and inspiration, it is a living joy. When effected without enough care and creativity, it is an enigmatic bore.

IV. UNEXPECTED BENEFITS

The economies of building a small house are self-evident. The aesthetic distillation possible in a small house presents wonderful opportunities for the designer. The functional efficiencies of condensed work spaces also save time and effort in the actual use of the house. But there are happy benefits that are not immediately obvious.

First and foremost is the benefit of energy efficiency. Superinsulation, air locks, solar orientation, eave design, and various air-moving and sun-shading technologies all help mitigate the cost of cooling or heating a building. But the simplest and most effective way to reduce heating and cooling costs of a house is via the reduction of the volume of air to be treated. Small houses better afford cross ventilation for cooling. Small houses also have less area to be artificially illuminated and allow for better solar penetration for natural lighting.

Second, the cause of innovation is well served in designing and living in a small home. Rather than look to a book of standards, the designer and occupant must rethink the very nature of all the typical givens, be it bathroom layout, laundry location, or techniques of storage.

Third, any site is better served when a building's footprint can be scaled down to use the best aspects of the site to full advantage. It is always easier to expand a building's impact by nonarchitectural means (walls, plantings, grade changes) than to rework a bloated building to fit a given site. This is especially true for the "problem site," where access, view, solar utility, or natural terrain force the house location into an inevitable compromise.

Last, long-term economies are effected when a scaled-down house is built. Obviously, lower building costs create lower financing costs, and energy efficiency greatly lowers the long-term cost of occupancy. But another long-term economy can be effected by reducing the size of the building to be built, and thus providing funds for the sort of materials and detailing that prevent long-term maintenance problems. A red cedar roof on 1 $\times$ 3 inch sheathing lasts twice as long as an asphalt shingle roof. Stonework needs little maintenance compared to wooden fences and concrete walks and steps. Wood paneling and tile work may never need refinishing during a typical 20-year occupancy, whereas paint and vinyl tile most assuredly will. In addition to the basic satisfaction of long-term maintenance savings, all these steps afford a certain visceral gratification as well.

V. METHODS AND RULES

As does any type of construction, the typical American home has traditional rules, both implicit and explicit, for its design. Traditionally, a "better" home has meant a bigger home. As affluence spread, storage space began to assert its impact on the American house plan with a vengeance. Fully one-third of the square footage was devoted to uninhabitable storage and circulation space. Also, rooms began to be added for discrete functions that once shared common living space. As the typical American home grew to embrace the "den," "rumpus room," "family room," and "library" as valued selling points, the average home began to feel the effects of unlimited spatial consumption.

Then, two nonarchitectural events intervened. First, two major energy crises boosted the heating and cooling costs of these newly bloated homes to the point of unaffordability. Second, the rise in real interest rates made big-ticket construction budgets simply unfeasible for the vast majority of home owners. The immediate responses to these economic inhibitors were the condominium and the cooperative—essentially, purchased apartments that afford tax advantages and some sense of ownership. But these dwellings have all the disadvantages of shared living environments—minimal personal space, communal rules, common walls, and spatial constriction—without any personal involvement in the design of the unit.

So it is with the sense of reorienting the priorities of the typical home owner that some architects have begun to explore seriously the possibilities of the small house as an uncompromising, personally integrated design. The goal is to create a freestanding home on its own lot for the cost of a comparable condominium. Obviously a trade-off of space for personalized possession must be effected.

It is in that spirit of reinvention versus a depressing diminution of expectation and hope that I present this list of basic revisionist thinking. None of the "rules" given here are new or magic, but when they are applied consistently to create delightful and efficient small houses, their value is enhanced.

Ease the Squeeze: Rules of Thumb

The Distant Prospect.   By situation a house can dominate and define a site, while its form can convey a power and impact far in excess of its true size. If the house is used as an endpoint in a long-range view or a definitive object in a natural space, the building can seem to control its surroundings and gain perceived stature.

Scale—The Most Valuable Tool

> *Exterior.*   To diffuse the singular identity of the small-house form is to dilute its potential. The basic image of the house form must be dominant and obvious. In other words, do not put the clear light of a small house under the bushel basket of diffusing exterior articulation of form.

> *Interior.*   Create extreme contrasts in scale using axes, cross axes, and the vertical dimension as larger-than-expected elements stand in sharp distinction to the tightly designed storage, bathroom, and kitchen spaces. If the budget allows, use detailing to enrich the entire composition by adding a depth of design to the very personal level—via mill work, furniture, lighting, etc.

Fenestration.   Essentially the same rules as above apply. By varying scale from larger than normal down to smaller than normal, you create a sense of rich contrast and enhance the individual door and window identities. But there is one simple proviso in the area of fenestration: There is no room in a small house for gratuitous glazing or entries. Each portal is precious, and because of its enhanced impact, due to the reduced amount of construction, the element must have a great deal of thought behind its design. Hence a single custom element such as a front door can transform the entire image of a house.

Roof.   This is perhaps the single most important formal element—with concurrent spatial implications. A small-house roof must be the indication of its essential plan. To create more than two basic roof elements is to muddy the perceptual waters to the point of confusion. Broad eaves reinforce the power of the roof as cap to a simple volume below. Flat roofs on small houses can create a sense of truncation rather than horizontal flow: often there is simply not enough house to provide the flowing effect.

The Vertical Dimension.   This is the most ignored tool for spatial sense in residential architecture. The simple breaking of the standard 8-foot ceiling height causes the eye and head to rise, and with them the spirit. The condensing of functions is tolerated much more easily in a loftier space.

Materials.   Use those materials that generate the most home-owner pride and that will require as little long-term maintenance as possible. Quality "reads" in most people's eyes. Aluminum siding, asphalt shingles, and textured plywood are forever compromises, imitations of the genuine articles. Conversely, high-quality or custom fenestration adds a sense of care and design that no occupant can ignore (especially given the energy efficiencies and maintenance savings that often result).

Space.   By definition, space is the most difficult dilemma in the small house. A fundamental distinction must be made between perceived and real square footage. The very nature of the axes and the use of the vertical dimension recommended in this list help excite the occupants by showing up their expectations to be merely assumptions based on previous experience. In order to create the luxuries of axial orientation and vertical spatial release, two basic methods of obtaining spatial relief must be implemented. First, thorough design with intimate owner involvement and a willingness to reinvent the wheel can result in much tighter organization of the kitchen, bath, and work areas. Second, exterior spaces can release warm-weather spatial squeeze, and perceptual relief can be realized by large-scale openings to those outdoor areas that are defined naturally or as part of the extended house (decks and patios).

Individual Elements. Stairs, beds, fireplaces, desks, and interior glazing can all follow the rules of reinterpretation by their considered application. Intrusions can be minimized, efficiencies effected, and delight enhanced simply by the willingness of the designer and client to rethink assumptions inbred over decades of conditioned response to typical problems in residential architecture.

Exterior Appliqués. Often the latent geometries of a house can be easily extended by the creative application of large-scale exterior elements such as stickwork, roof overhangs, pergolas, or gardens. Not overtly ornamental, these elaborations can serve to greatly aggrandize a project without enormous expense.

If there is one abiding rule, one singular objective, it is to *create* renewed delight and surprise by the *reduction* of the space to be built. The only way to insure a painless reduction of scale in a dwelling is to have a dialogue between dedicated architect and open home owner. In the rethinking of so many basic assumptions by the home owner and architect, an important secondary benefit of personal insight is realized.

Rather than adapting their lives to their accommodations, home owners can reinvent their dwellings to serve their reexamined lifestyles. The resulting sense of personal empowerment engenders the sort of pride and commitment no decorated condominium can match.

VI. CONCLUSION

Given the socioeconomic dominance of the baby boom generation as it grows into full familyhood, the present state of ad hoc accommodations must change.

Multiple-family approaches to housing can relieve some of the short-term accommodation needs. Unfortunately, the home, being the largest single investment of the vast majority of people, demands more consumer satisfaction than simple utility.

The opportunity to create high-quality, high-art homes at costs comparable to those of condominium units has begun to be addressed in recent years. Obviously there is no free lunch, and given the latent economies of multiple-unit construction, the freestanding home must be reduced in size to be competitive in the marketplace.

To reduce its size and maintain its desirability, the small house must be a thoughtfully designed, thoroughly efficient building, containing the appointments and amenities that foster pride in ownership. The only way to achieve this end is via the use of talented architects.

This book presents the tip of a growing iceberg. Traditionally designed as vacation homes, second homes, carriage houses, starter homes, or retirement homes, the architect-designed small house in America is graduating to a new role, that of a primary component in the lexicon of general-use housing.

It is only by demonstrated success that the architect-designed small house can prove itself to be the viable alternative to continued domestic frustration. This book has been compiled to show the state of the art in small-house design. In a great many ways, it is intended to show that good things do indeed come in small packages.

A Connecticut House

A prototype

It would be very easy simply to parade pretty pictures of diminutive houses across the pages of this book and state that exposure was complete. However, if the opportunity is missed to convey a deeper sense of what potential economies can be realized through small-house design, then the truths stated remain unproved.

Fortunately this author has spent the better part of 2 years translating ideas into a specific built form. Given the intimacy of involvement, a certain lack of objectivity must be forgiven in exchange for the amount of knowledge that is to be communicated.

Mick Hales

The Dickinson House

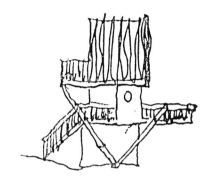

LIST OF PARTICULARS

Location:	Madison, Connecticut	
Space:	Finished, heated	1100 square feet
	Defined, unheated (deck, carport, entry)	800 square feet
	Total perceived*	1800 square feet
Costs:	Lot	$ 28,500
	Construction only	65,000
	Site work	7,000
	Appliances	3,000
	Total project cost	$103,500**

*See page 27 for methodology.

**Does not include architect's fee; note that project is owner-painted.

Architect: Duo Dickinson

Contractor: Post Road Wood Products

I n 1982 the Dickinsons, an architect and soon-to-be law student, decided that the central material focus in their lives was their home. In this case the home did not exist—but its vision was the single most important aspect of their material wants and desires.

Unfortunately, because the Dickinsons were in their late twenties, cash was far from a readily available commodity. They desired an in-town location in a coastal Connecticut town, and lots were either occupied by centuries-old homes or outrageously priced.

The first lot they inspected was well-situated but difficult to build on, and the price was simply prohibitive. Many other lots were walked, pondered, and rejected because they were too remote or too expensive or because there were too many questions about resale value.

After more than a year and a half of searching, the Dickinsons found that the original lot remained unsold. They made an offer far below the original asking price, negotiations were held, and satisfaction was reached.

The lot represents the ugly-duckling bargain that only a trained eye can see as having swan potential. A list of restrictions and problems reads as follows:

1. The lot was in a coastal wetlands-management area; therefore:

   • Any basement would have to be designed to resist hydrostatic loading—and would be quite expensive to build.

   • The septic field would also have to be engineered and constructed carefully—and quite expensively.

   • The first-floor height had to be at least 20 feet above area high water.

2. Vehicular and utility access to the site was over a 200-foot right-of-way; therefore:

   • Cars could access the site itself at only one point at the edge of a steep drop.

   • Utility lines had to traverse over 100 feet through rock-ledge, again increasing costs.

3. There was very poor passive solar potential. The site was essentially a hillside facing a northerly 6-acre salt marsh. Winter sunlight was indirect until the mid-morning

hours, and the primary view orientation was due north, with no potential for solar gain.

4. Since the lot was a subdivision of the backyard of an existing house, the owners of that house were the sellers, and they did not want their view restricted. Hence a sight line was determined as the point behind which all building could happen.

5. The proximity to the sellers' house was a problem. The sellers' house was a looming Shingle Style building. Aesthetically its nearness had to be addressed; functionally, its visual intrusion had to be avoided.

6. There was a steep drop-off at the site edge. If a normal home with yard and garage was to be accommodated, huge quantities of fill had to be brought in.

The site presented many negative aspects. Obviously a typical raised ranch house, Cape Cod cottage, or saltbox would be economically foolhardy in terms of the amount of site work needed. The wonderful salt-marsh view was obscured by lush undergrowth. The utility companies' estimates for hookups were outrageously expensive.

Amid all this adversity was a vision held by the architect, which led to a singular design concept. Three grand old white oaks stood on the site. From early morning until sunset, light struck their upper trunks and all their limbs. Seeing this simple fact, the architect saw the potential for a different type of "raised" house. If a simple method for raising the house could be provided, the crucial problem of poor solar penetration could be solved and the mandatory first-floor elevation could be effected without excessive landfill costs.

Utility-access costs could be greatly reduced if all blasting costs were directly assumed by the home owners, bypassing the bloated utility-company estimates. The other site restrictions and limitations could be dealt with— as long as optimism and a tight budget spurred on creativity.

As the photographs and drawings best illustrate, this is a simple house made special by its situation—held aloft by two bearing walls—and by the articulation of its various parts. The system-by-system description that follows enhances the images shown.

Figures 1–7 *The construction process. A platform, made rigid by gussetted knee braces, supports walls, which in turn support sheathing and then a roof. All is clad in insulation and shingles, the finish trim is painted, and the stonework buttresses are completed. All steps involve simple-span symmetrical framing and standard techniques used in thoughtful ways. (Figures continue on pages 11 and 12.)*

1

Photos 1–6 courtesy of the architect

CONSTITUENT SYSTEMS

1. *Structure*

   - *Foundation.* There are two bearing walls with buttressed end conditions, plus continuous triangulated stiffening (in the form of framing) at the top edges of the walls.

   - *Framing.* Floors and roof 2 × 10s, 16 inches on center; walls are made of 2 × 4s, 16 inches on center; triangulating bracing made of 2 × 6s with ¾ inch plywood gussetts at the corners.

   - *Beams.* Two composite beams consisting of four 2 × 10s run the entire length of the house, terminating to the north as cantilevered support for the deck.

   - *Sheathing.* On all exterior walls and on the north and south interior walls of the living room, ½ inch plywood was used, creating shear walls. Wood sheathing (1 × 3s) was used on the roof.

   - *Steel.* Reinforcing bars were used throughout all concrete work, and an 18-foot, 6 × 6 steel angle was used to stiffen the living room's north wall. Also, ¾-inch steel tie-rods were used to prevent roof sag at the spring point of the cathedral ceiling.

2. *Insulation.* All exterior wall and floor cavities were filled with maximum-depth fiberglass batt insulation, with vapor barrier; all exterior walls and underside were covered with ¾ inch urethane sheathing (this meets U.S. Department of Housing and Urban Development guidelines for the region). Note that the living area serves as a de facto insulating air bag when not in use.

3. *Exterior Surfaces.* Roof and walls are covered with clear red cedar shingles, 6 inches to weather. All corners are mitred, and there is an 8-inch band of white cedar shingles, bordered by two 2-inch red cedar clapboards (1 inch to weather each). Underside and eaves are made of painted poplar 6-inch tongue and groove. Trim is made of clear cedar, painted.

3

4

4. *Interior Surfaces*

- All walls are made of ½-inch gypsum board, painted.

- The first-story floor is made of 6-inch poplar, urethaned.

- The bedroom floor and the steps are carpeted.

- The bath has a mosaic tile floor and wainscot.

- The kitchen and bath ceilings are made of painted poplar 6-inch tongue and groove; other ceilings are made of ½-inch gypsum board.

- All trim is made of painted poplar.

5. *Heating.* The house is heated with gas-fired hot water, using radiator (versus baseboard) distribution. Note that the solar orientation of the south end of the house and the use of a fireplace in the living room aid in heating. Note also that the clothes drier vents internally and that the vents for the heating plant, hot-water heater, and chimney flue run inside the house, all allowing gain.

6. *Plumbing.* There is a single vent stack and a vertical chase.

7. *Electricity.* The house has standard 100-ampere service, expandable to 200 amperes.

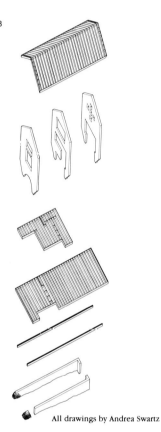

8

All drawings by Andrea Swartz

Figure 8 *Exploded structural axonometric. Two end-buttress bearing walls support single-direction floor framing. The second floor is essentially a loft set between two of the three shear walls designed to keep the structure rigid. The roof is a symmetrical simple-span structure held tight by the shear walls and three steel tie-rods.*

5

6

7

Mick Hales

THE HOUSE ITSELF

Aesthetes and nonaesthetes have described this house as a "covered bridge," "doghouse," "car wash," and "ark." The simple truth is that this house is the direct result of two interfacing systems.

Essentially those systems are the built parts (the structure) and the applied parts (the inserted elements, such as doors, windows, cabinet work, mill work, lighting, and plumbing).

There were inherent limitations in building this house—not the least of which was a modest budget ($65,000 to $70,000 for construction), but there were equally inherent means to defeat the sense of limits. The house was to have an extremely simple occupancy (a married couple), and it would be built with an adventurous spirit born of the home owners' relative youth (27 at the beginning of the project).

The owners hoped to use existing technologies for construction to reduce the complexity of fabrication while creating a fresh sense of space and form with innovative applications of those very same standard building techniques.

To help define the internal dynamism of familiar systems used in interpretive ways, let us turn to a discussion of the rationales behind the two systems, built and applied.

The Constructed House

In contemplating a small prototypical house, famous architects of the past and present have sought to reinvent the methods used to design and build small structures. Whether it is Gropius and his grid/frame, Frank Lloyd Wright and his hexagonal or circular grids, Le Corbusier and his Modulor, or Buckminster Fuller and his geodesic dome, the heroic designer of the past has inspired contemporaries and future admirers.

Unfortunately none of the average houses built in the United States today use the techniques developed by such designers, primarily because the architect-applied materials, techniques, or dimensioning systems involved are thoroughly uncoordinated with the existing building technology that has been in use since the late ninteenth century. The architects, some of this era, some of the past, who have advocated everything from air-inflated structures to urethane foam shells to recycled beer cans set in concrete as methods of construction have ignored one simple historical truth: A concept becomes the status quo only when its utility is proved over time.

Standardized use of dimension lumber (2 × 4s, 2 × 6s, 2 × 8s, etc.) and the 16-inch module that progresses into 4 × 8 foot sheets of material is simply a fait accompli in the building trade. To ignore this fact and invent a new system simply prevents that new system from having economic viability for the vast majority of American homes.

So the dimensioning, form, and structural detailing of the Dickinson house have been based on the use of standard building materials and the 16-inch framing module, plus several essential cost-saving applications of that technology. Presented in the form of a list, here are the various uses familiar framing technology has been put to, maximizing its economy by reinforcing its latent simplicity.

1. *Length of Building.* Determined by 16-inch framing module.

2. *Width of Building.* Determined by uncut 20-foot-long 2 × 10 joists. (Note that 20 feet is fifteen 16-inch modules.)

3. *Location of Foundation Walls.* Placed at maximum span (12 feet) and cantilever (4 feet) of 2 × 10 joists noted above.

4. *Straight-Run Stairs.* No platforms or winders.

5. *No Curved Walls.* The only curves present in the house are in the form of cut surfaces (south wall opening, countertops).

6. *Standard Roof Pitch (8 in 12).* This accommodates prefabricated vent flue flashing.

7. *Symmetrical Roof Framing.* No valleys, dormers, changes in pitch, or crickets.

8. *Single-Direction Framing.* All loads bear directly on foundation walls; there are no load-bearing and -collecting beams or columns.

9. *No Crenellations in House Form.* All formal variation is via *reduction* from the building perimeter derived by 20-foot joist and 16-inch framing module.

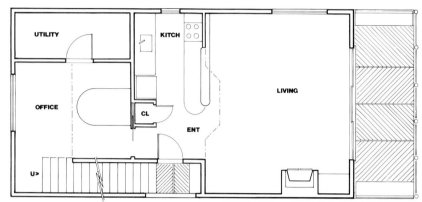

Figure 9 *First floor. The entry axis through the kitchen is counterpointed by the grand axis extending the entire length of the house. A generous living room (right) has an applied deck addressing the salt-marsh view, while a "career room" (left) serves as a convection space above which sits the bedroom. Note that the utility room/basement stakes out the southwest corner of the house.*

9

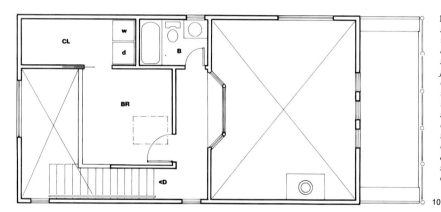

Figure 10 *Second floor. The open space on either side of the bedroom makes it appear to "float." The closet and bath vertically extend the service zone which is defined on the first floor by the utility room. Note the common utility chase between washer-dryer and tub. Note also the use of the standard bay window to separate the two heating zones. The entire northern portion of the house is given over to the living room, creating an expansive space and an air-bag insulating space for the southerly portion of the house, more often used in the winter months.*

10

Figure 11 *Section. This section evidences the two spatial and environmental zones facing west. The southerly bedroom-study (left) and the northerly kitchen–living room (right) interlock at the corridor and bay window extension. Note the balcony posture of the bedroom and the low-wall division of the kitchen from the living area. Note also the tiny attic pinched between the north and south portions of the house, and how its imposition above the central hall creates the one horizontally focused space in the house.*

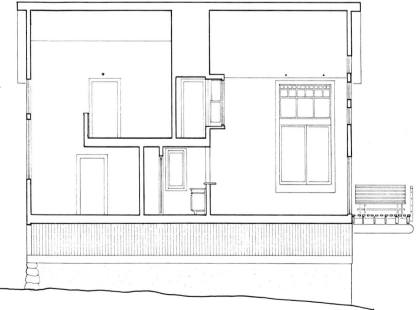

11

The Applied Parts

As with the construction techniques discussed above, those items that are inserted into and applied onto the structural frame can be viewed as opportunities for finding delight in redefining existing technology. A chief selling point to architect-designed residences is their level of finish. This is due to better use of higher-quality materials and components.

The counterpoint to the sense of care in the detailing of architect-designed buildings is the seemingly devil-may-care attitude about certain crucial functional aspects of the detailing.

First and foremost of the unfortunate truths about architect-designed homes is that skylights, custom glazing, and awkward flashing conditions all tend to invite leaks. Second, seamless aesthetics employed in Modernist architecture are anathema to the natural world of expansion and contraction, corrosion and use. Last, custom-designed and -crafted items are all untested; hence, they may prove to be dysfunctional over time more often than standard products.

But if innovation were always ignored for the safety of the familiar, this would be a book about the small cave. The choice is not simply between impractical innovation and stultifying mundanity; there is a middle ground of prioritized points of customization versus wholesale standardization.

When this book's introduction dealt with using the exciting dynamics of scale as a means to liberate the small house from aesthetic inertia, windows and doors were crucial aspects of that interplay. Similarly, locations of all applied parts should harmonize with the structural module discussed, and these objects should be placed to reinforce dominant views, axes, and spatial organizations. Here is a listing of those objects that helped create the lively spirit of the Dickinson house.

1. *Windows.* Windows were oriented to specific views and light conditions (south, north, and west). Larger windows are best for light and view, smaller ones for ventilation, backlighting, and small spaces. All of these guidelines can *reduce* the total number of windows in a house, and hence the cost, while they *increase* energy efficiency and aesthetic impact.

2. *Doors.* The number of doors needed was minimized by creating multiple-purpose spaces. A door can be used to release the power of an axis (as in the Dickinson entry).

3. *Custom Items.* The following custom items were used to reinforce the overriding qualities of the spaces they are situated in: mouldings, cabinet work, work station, upper window units (south and west), front door, deck benches and bollards, front steps, range hood, handrails, fireplace moulding, living room shelf, and bay window underside.

4. *Standard Items, Used Reinterpretively.* In the Dickinson house, you find an interior bay window, sliding doors used as windows, standard tile patterned creatively, and a prefabricated firebox used in a special way. All of these create custom-quality amenity at no more cost than that of the catalog components these items truly are.

5. *Lighting.* The number of lighting fixtures needed was minimized through impact-conscious use.

6. *Oddball Catalog Items.* Radiators, sink faucet, bath hardware, lighting—all add a sense of delight to potentially bland settings without the cost of custom fabrication.

7. *Paint.* With the use of four tones, from white to light yellow, portions of the house were highlighted, enhancing latent intricacies and formal identities at no additional cost, save time to the owners, who painted the house themselves.

By taking nothing for granted, you can use proven technologies—economical in both purchase price and installation cost—for the interior finishing of a house, and you can use them in innovative ways to reinforce the basic organization and aesthetics of the house. In the Dickinson house, a mix of custom, standard, and imaginatively reinterpreted items has been used to add depth to an otherwise simplistic house.

Similarly, for construction the most familiar of building technologies—standard lightweight frame construction—was used in such a direct manner that the subtractive manipulations of the exterior form derived enormous power.

Now that the site restrictions encountered and the building techniques employed have been discussed, it is time to assess the latent organizational and aesthetic intentions of the Dickinson house.

THE HOUSE AS A WHOLE
Meanings and Intentions

Perched on a hillside amid four large trees, a small (20 × 38 feet) rectangular form achieves grandeur by elevation above the slope. A simple two-story, extruded-gable form swells above a reduced foundation plinth.

The actual broad-stroke detailing of the house—roof pitch, surface detailing, and essential spirit—was keyed to the immediately adjacent Shingle Style house. A positive ambiguity was effected through conscientious referencing without mimicry. Perhaps a retrofitted carriage house, or just a somewhat bizarre architectural offspring, the house creates an implicit entry court by filling in the void between existing house and garage, while being centered on the existing driveway.

The maximum impact is derived by using the swelled, lofty intentions of the house in the most direct manner. A sense of articulation in the context of a prosaic form is achieved by emphasizing the local symmetries of the gable ends while effecting ad hoc facade compositions on the side elevations. The blanket of red cedar shingles covering the exterior is allowed to dominate certain areas of the house, while a white cedar shingle datum around its entire girth and reduced spacing at the south-facade peak violate the continuity just enough to avoid a sense of unrelenting dominance.

The use of a multitude of scales—from the dominant form to unexpectedly large windows to shingle detailing (and all the steps in between)—allows visual excitement to prevail over predictability.

Identities, personal and architectural, come in a variety of sizes. The nature of the small house can constrict the identities of the parts presented by any house. In the Dickinson house the scale differential is exaggerated via the use of broad expanses of shingles, highly varied fenestration, and subsequently sized trim. This creates an articulate dialogue between the simple house form and the necessary violations of the building's envelope.

Internally, spatial identities are reinforced by limiting the intentions. Because 90 percent of the storage space is condensed into two large closets and a small attic, the four remaining rooms are allowed to express themselves without undue stress on the small scale of the house itself.

12

Photos 12–27 by Mick Hales

13

14

15

16

Figure 12 *Entry. A centered "face" greets the arriving occupant-to-be. The entry creates the natural focus for the preexisting driveway. (Facing page.)*

Figure 13 *(above) Northwest. A lofted, extruded-gable form is wrapped in cedar shingles to effect a simple, powerful presence. Extreme scalar manipulation of windows helps activate the exterior visually, while a continuous band of white cedar shingles act as a datum to all the fenestration activity. Note the applied parts of the deck and the outsize trim work painted white to contrast with the ubiquitous natural materials.*

Figure 14 *Entry. The east facade has poor access to the sun and little view, so its form can easily accommodate an expressive stair and entry. Note how the painted tongue-and-groove underbelly contrasts with the cedar skin. The entry stairs are expressively detailed to provide some creative construction in spite of the code-compliant floor height. Note how the easterly hole (upper right) and extended corner (lower left) help create the sense of an animated skin. Extended trim widths, painted joist, and considered door and window location create an active array of parts amid the sea of cedar.*

Figure 15 *Bench, exterior. Deck seating serves double duty as a barrier and triple duty as an aesthetically active piece opposed to the house's mass. Note the turned bollard used for deck restraint. All materials used are weather-resistant (redwood, teak, and clear cedar), allowing for a minimum of maintenance.*

Figure 16 *Bench, from deck. A civilized composition of parts both restrains and accommodates.*

The entry to the house site presents the symmetrical south facade. A detached (though enclosed) entry stair beckons upward to a landing. It pierces the shingle fabric, leading into an inner wall-covering system of painted tongue and groove.

Opposite the glass front door, the first overt axis (across the short direction of the house) presents itself as people enter. The axis works in both directions—coming and going: The galley of the kitchen, the tongue-and-groove ceiling extended from the entry, the centered window opposite the front door, and the large wall opening behind the front door are defining elements.

What is perceived as a main axis on entry is revealed to be simply a cross axis upon occupancy. The major axis of the house occurs along the entire 38-foot length available in the house form. Framed at one end by one bay of the sliding glass door unit and bollard rail supports beyond, and rewarded at the other end by the lightly celebrational stair bottom, this axis not surprisingly both directs traffic and provides a grand-scale element unexpected in an 1100-square-foot house.

There is a single dominant space encountered in a promissory way upon entry. The living-dining, semi-Great Hall area is the cathedral of the house itself; its unintentionally reverential cruciform clerestory glazing pattern receives the raised expectations encountered. A sweeping 12-foot sliding glass door opening onto a generous deck captures the full horizontal view of the 6-acre salt marsh, while the vertical window array to the west captures the ascending form of a nearby maple.

The windows used—centered cruciform clerestory, horizontal slider, and vertical array—present a catalog of basic window orientations. These windows are set amid broad planes of painted wall surfaces, with one tone for the gable end, another for the side walls, and a third for the ceiling. Wood floors add a large-scale organic surface amid all the paint.

17

Figure 17 *Entry. A custom front door allows morning light to flood kitchen (right). Custom mouldings wrap all openings. Note carpet edge signaling stair (center). Note also the extension of painted tongue-and-groove material inside to the kitchen ceiling from the exterior entry. Note last the extra luster provided by the latch sets applied to the doors.*

Figure 18 *Kitchen and entry view. Simple, inexpensive cabinets are opposed to create a galley kitchen. The axis created between the cabinets centers upon the front door and orients the radiator and window as well. Teak counters and a custom range hood enliven the entry vantage.*

18

19

Figure 19 *Living room, west. This ensemble of openings is the visual greeting the house provides once the occupant proceeds over the threshold. The westerly tall window is a duplicate of the window first apprehended upon access to the site. Made from a standard slide below and custom fixed unit above, the glazing division mimics the tree form opposite it, while the window's shape captures both the intense sunsets and the tree's ascendancy. The horizontal slider affords an uninterrupted sweep of the salt-marsh view. The cluster of square clerestory windows above (which forms a cruciform when fully depicted) is a centered array providing both ambient light and ventilation. The vertical, horizontal, and centered fenestration provide a minor-league compendium of the orientations possible in any glazing system. Note the tie-rod orientation to the west window, which in turn is oriented to the fireplace opposite, creating a minor subaxis.*

Figure 20 *Fireplace. The least expensive fireplace available is made special by applied parts. Note the orientation of the tie-rods to the chimney. The fireplace is the single major formal event within the living room, counterpointing the outscaled space. Note that the windowless easterly wall provides a blank background for these activities.*

Figure 21 *Living room, south. A dialogue between the kitchen void below and the expressive bay window above is effected with a considered application of a variety of lighting and texture. The bay window underside has some custom detailing applied to catch light and provide finish. A sense of the major axis can be seen in the ongoing corridor to the left. Note the ubiquitous poplar flooring.*

Figure 22 *Work room. With the bedroom loft above, a large-scale niche accommodates a simple partner's desk for a young author-architect and his law-student wife. The column support for the desk, the ziggurat light, and the wrapping mouldings all provide a sense of quiet articulation and expression.*

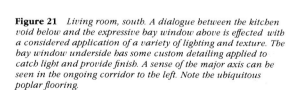

20 The Small House

Perhaps the single most surprising element in the room is the interior bay window applied to the south wall, centered in the gable. This large-scale standard exterior element presents a positive intrusion into the double-height space, producing a focal point where one is thoroughly needed. Additionally, magenta-painted tie-rods, hung lights, and fan all conspire to add life and scale to the rather lofty north-facing space.

The major positive element in this sea of space is the fireplace. Overtly objectified (versus integrated), it has a larger-than-furniture scale to add a formal focus on axis with the vertical window array. When tie-rods, flue, and hung lights all follow this same axis, a second secondary ordering datum is created, helping to subdivide a potentially awkward room.

The kitchen is designed to condense storage and provide maximum utility in a small space. A not-so-low low wall provides visual linkage but allows perceptual distinction. The kitchen and living spaces form the now-standard functional couplet of "serving and served" and are the north-oriented, view-responsive portions of the house.

The south, solar-oriented part contains a "career zone" work area on the first floor along with the storage utility room—which functions as the basement in this elevated house.

Above these two utilitarian spaces are the twin private sections of the house. Bedroom and bath offer no inkling of their presence until one ascends the stair. Here, the third subaxis in the house is presented, in the form of the upstairs corridor—aligned with the bath door and sink, with the window and light at its terminus.

In the bath itself, a subtle tile pattern, cathedralized ceiling of painted tongue-and-groove material (allusive to the entry), and teak appointments are used to create an intimacy of detail that embraces its occupants.

In the bedroom, the gable end center is used to orient the bed to the custom upper windows of the south array. As in the living room, a lighting fixture, fan, and tie-rod add scale and delight from above. A large prefabricated skylight releases the eyes of the bed resident and provides indirect morning light and perfect summer ventilation. The bedroom is indeed the pilothouse of the Dickinson home, using its house-centered posture to create the seat of personal power.

The second storage room, in the form of a walk-in closet and laundry, feeds off the bedroom. A high level of density is achieved by using the vertical space available.

A note on expansion: Small houses may not remain small forever. Adding to the Dickinson house takes on two scenarios, planned by the architect. The first scheme involves internal addition only. The east portion of the living room over the fireplace can easily accommodate a child's bedroom, creating an inglenook around the fireplace. Similarly, the "basement" utility room can have a half bath inserted into its space. Internal addition is quite painless, using all existing structural support and leaving exterior surfaces untouched, save for a moved window or two. The second scenario (involving a longer occupancy and more money) would be to build a freestanding tower to the east—connected at the top of the stairs only—which would house two bedrooms and a bath. Since presently there is no glazing to the northeast, no existing view would be obstructed, and similarly the westerly septic field and sight-line restriction would be respected.

23

Figure 23 *Loft and stair. A large-scale, positive form is revealed within the simple envelope of the house. Tie-rod, light, and skylight beckon (upper left) while the stair focuses upon the low-ceiling corridor. Note the window-muntin shadows cast upon the loft front, and the openings at the top of the interior wall (center), which provide natural illumination to the stair itself.*

Figure 24 *Bedroom. Juxtaposed elements are cut into or are applied upon the planes described, while other items sit in the open space defined.*

Figure 25 *Bedroom ceiling, bed-bound prospect. Not unlike the dangling toys in an infant's crib mobile, these elements—structural, utilitarian, and whimsical—float under the arching ceiling and yet defer to the centered focus of the room, the custom fixed window of the south wall (left).*

A Connecticut House   **23**

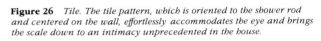

26

Figure 26 *Tile. The tile pattern, which is oriented to the shower rod and centered on the wall, effortlessly accommodates the eye and brings the scale down to an intimacy unprecedented in the house.*

Figure 27 *Bath. Window, light, and sink center on the doorway opposite, which in turn addresses the hall beyond; all the orientations create a sense of accommodation. Note that the tile, teak, cathedralized ceiling, and fixtures all help to enliven a tiny room.*

27

THE HOUSE AS A PROTOTYPE

The question remains, is this house merely a nice idiosyncratic project, evolved of personal preference, or does it have lessons for the general art of small-house design?

The answer to each question, for this house and all the projects in this book, is yes. With an atypical site and an owner-architect, this is not an average scenario. But my contention is that the difficulty of the topography and wetlands conditions balances the relative flexibility of having an owner-architect.

Similarly, the benefit of the absence of an architect's fee (in this case determined as 15 percent of $65,000, or $9750) could be balanced by the use of small-scale (⅛ inch equals 1 foot) drawings done for a fixed fee, which would be offered by this particular architect, for example, for $3000.

The plethora of custom-designed elements can be seen as indulgent lily-gilding, which could be eliminated to cut costs

Other than landscaping and painting by the owners, this house was built on the basis of a contract with a general contractor, with the owner purchasing some appliances directly and installing some oddball items personally.

Given that no two projects are alike, the Dickinson house represents a clear image of the dance between the standard and the lyric. If you simplify the most common framing techniques and apply them in a manner that facilitates creative adaptation, you can find the innovative possibilities inherent in the standard.

It is hoped that the photos of this house and the principles set forth in the introduction dovetail to the point of mutual reinforcement. A small house needn't be intimidated by its size, and it needn't try to be anything more than a simple dwelling.

It is in finding the harmony between utility, construction, and art that architecture grows beyond the simply servile. The intangible elements of form, scale, detail, and space can be manipulated so thoroughly in a small house that there are no excuses for the architect except a failure of imagination.

The following pages show the manifest implementations of the basic precepts discussed in the introduction. If a common thread of thought is present and reinforced by these words, then so much the better for all those people seeking to reward their hard work and nesting instincts with thoughtful, affordable homes.

COST-SAVING ASPECTS ENUMERATED

1. No basement
2. No gutters, leaders, or perimeter drains
3. No curving walls
4. Minimized number of windows and doors
5. Straight-run stairs, no winders or platforms
6. No flashing, save at flue penetration of roof, and standard drip caps over doors and windows
7. One bathroom
8. Single utility chase
9. Single-direction framing—no load-collecting beams or columns
10. Symmetrical volume—no eccentric loading, hence no beams
11. Maximum utilization of structural properties of framing lumber (optimum span and cantilever)
12. Most importantly—*minimized* number of square feet built

A
Special
Note

The concept of perceptual space

W hen architects describe their projects to other architects, clients, or the media, they often use square footages to delineate the scale of their work. This book defines a small house as one of the following:

A one or two bedroom house with fewer than 2000 square feet

A three or four bedroom house with fewer than 2500 square feet

A five or more bedroom house with fewer than 3500 square feet

These criteria are based on standard practices of counting all heated space within perimeter walls as all of its nominal amount and counting all unheated space at one-half its nominal amount. Other factors allow for double-height space and other variations, but simply put, space is space, and its only use as quantified square footage in this book is for comparative purposes.

However, architects cheat to up the amount of reported square footage built to reduce the cost per square feet of the projects. The more they build for less, the more innovative and resourceful they appear in spending their clients' money.

In the presentation of these houses, the use of nominal figures alone would misrepresent the projects. I have attempted to offer an alternative to nominal square footages. I propose a secondary figure be presented, a figure ambiguously called "perceptual square footage." Since most square-footage figures are interpretive products, I propose to acknowledge that a building is *perceived* not *measured.*

Two essential elements unacknowledged in nominal-square-footage calculation are axes and double-height spaces. Since these elements are used in the recalculation, definitions are needed.

Axis. An axis is a linear space linked visually through other spaces, with a beginning and an end defined by incidence with an aligned element—door, window, stair, fireplace, etc. Axes are often corridors, or subdividing, orienting alignments in larger rooms.

Double-Height Space. Double-height space is space that is 10 or more feet high, before any cathedralizing ceiling angling. Note that for ease of calculation, no recognition of ceiling peak height is considered in this formula.

Secondly, small architecturally defined exterior spaces directly integrated into the house plan—decks, patios, porches—should be acknowledged, but unoccupiable space not visible from the interior of the house should not.

THE FORMULA

Axes

Since axes are often perceived *and* utilized, all axes, as separable plan elements, are counted twice.

Example: The Dickinson house has one major axis, which is 3.5 × 38 feet, and three subaxes—kitchen; living room (fireplace and west window); and second-floor corridor—all assumed at 3 × 20 feet. The total added square feet would equal:

$$(3.5 \times 38) + 3 (3 \times 20) = 313 \text{ square feet}$$

Double-Height Space

The second house-expanding perceived space does not increase usable floor area but should be counted. Since all space has its major impact upon entry and since vertically enhanced space relies on the diagonal perception along sight lines across rooms, all spaces with a wall height of 10 feet or more should be perceptually sized as the true cross dimension at entry × the perceived diagonal to the maximum wall height. This *replaces* the normal length × width measurement in nominal computation; hence, there is a *net* gain.

Example: In the Dickinson house the living room and study area have two-story spaces. Normally, the living room would be calculated as 16 × 20 feet and the den as 13 × 12 feet for a total of 476 square feet. Figured as perceived square feet, the result is as follows:

Living room:

$$20 \text{ actual feet} \times 22 \text{ diagonal feet} = 440 \text{ square feet}$$

Study:

$$\text{Single-height portion} = 7 \times 12 \text{ feet} = 84 \text{ square feet}$$

$$\text{Double-height portion} = 12 \text{ actual feet} \times 21 \text{ diagonal feet} = 252 \text{ square feet}$$

The total number of perceived square feet in these rooms is 776. This represents a net increase of 300 square feet, or 40 percent.

Defined Space

All spaces defined architecturally but unheated or necessarily enclosed that are directly perceived from within the house should be acknowledged in the computation of perceived space. Since these spaces are usable only during fair weather, they are counted as half their nominal square feet.

Example: In the Dickinson house the entry deck (3.5 × 5 feet) and north deck (6.75 × 20 feet) would be counted as follows:

$$\frac{(3.5 \times 5) + (6.75 \times 20)}{2} = 76.25 \text{ square feet}$$

Unused Space

Carports and unheated utility spaces that have no functional utility save appliance storage and that are unperceived from the house should not be counted.

Example: In the Dickinson house the 450-square-foot carport would not be counted.

The Whole-House Example

Here are the results all factored into the Dickinson house.

Total nominal square feet, heated:	1100
Added areas:	
Axes	313
Double-height space (net increase)	300
Defined, unheated space	76
Total perceived square feet	1789 ±

It is hoped that as the perceived square footages are compared with the nominal figures for the projects presented, an enhanced sense of successful small-home design will be communicated.

THE
SINGLE-FAMILY
RESIDENCE

As described in the introduction, the greatest challenge to the profession of residential architecture lies in designing full-time residences that contain the elements, amenities, and detailing that evince pride in ownership while maintaining affordability.

Freestanding residences cannot compete economically with multiple-unit housing projects given the combined savings facilitated by large-scale construction, shared site access, and common utility hook ups. However, *architect-designed* freestanding homes can compensate for these disadvantages. An architect can design a house reduced in size, thereby increasing its efficiency and cost effectiveness.

The following house designs contain all the elements of human accommodation usually considered essential plus other concerns this book deems to be equally essential. Those particular design priorities focused upon are the innovations used to defeat the spatial squeeze imposed on houses that are comparably priced to their condominium counterparts. Whether one or ten sleeping spaces are accommodated, these homes have been subjected to reduced spatial consumption. "Small" is indeed a relative modifier, and the larger homes presented are small in their context.

Considered construction can evidence a set of priorities that mitigate the compromises necessitated when designing a downsized house. Unlike second homes or vacation homes, the following homes are inhabited on a full-time basis; therefore, the complete range of functional requirements must be met. Ongoing occupancy means that a house has to accommodate the open-ended truth of a family's evolution. Changing needs, growing numbers, and a full range of environmental influences must be dealt with effectively if a house design is to be successful.

A home is ultimately just a home, and the methods of designing small houses so that they are embracing beyond their true size are not magic, new, or revolutionary. However, when presented in the form of concerted efforts by dedicated professionals, a body of work can gain a reinforcing sense of aesthetic consistencies.

Particulars can give birth to general principles, and awareness of potentials can be heightened to inspire both potential home owners and architects alike. Housing in America today has been a study of dreams deferred, of the accepted reality of compromise, and of reduced expectation. Despite catastrophic interest rates, diminishing site availability, and spiraling construction costs, an intimately scaled house can break the assumed rules. However, without equivalent or heightened desirability, no freestanding home can hope to compete with an existing condominium or rental which is more affordable. Small houses, unapologetically conceived and executed as such, can meet the challenge of multiunit housing only when they are approached with an enlightened outlook. The design profession can have viable meaning to the average American household only when it can be shown to produce affordable homes of uncompromising utility and aesthetic delight.

The potential to do this has been tested and is displayed on the following pages, presented from smallest to least small. It is hoped that the promises made in this book's introduction are well met by the images shown.

Four Walls
and a Lot of Work

Buzz Yudell and Tina Beebe transform a shell into a house.

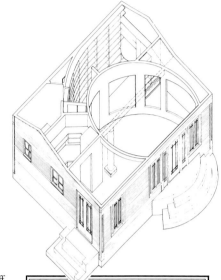

This is the only project in this book which is not a completely new, from-the-ground-up house. Other projects were rejected because they were indeed overt addendums to or renovations of existing buildings, and this author has an inkling that there are books available addressing the issues of residential renovation and addition.

What makes this project different from a straight renovation is that the existing building was not played off of; there was no aesthetic or formal input from the existing enclosure. Rather, this is a new house designed within a given perimeter. This situation is not unlike one in which an architect has his or her work defined by a structural bay or a design module, or one in which an architect finds that zoning laws impose a perimeter for a new house being built on an extremely tight site.

In this case the given perimeter was a 570-square-foot cottage in Santa Monica, California. As with many of the projects in this book, the budget was tight and the site was restrictive, but the designers—architect Buzz Yudell; his wife, Tina Beebe (a colorist and graphic designer); and John Ruble, Yudell's partner—had the imagination and wherewithal to defeat the perceived limits of the four walls they encountered. This is more or less an owner-built-and-designed project, and the effect obtained is extraordinary for the money invested.

The starting point was indeed a simple 22 × 28 foot rectangle, and the design response was equally straightforward.

The first and definitive step taken by the team was to impose a single large-scale element on the small-scale house design—an elliptic living space. Although superficially arbitrary, the

ARCHITECTS' STATEMENT

In an effort to cope with the staggering escalation of real estate costs, we joined with our partner John Ruble and his wife, Cathleen Stasz, to find a lot with two units. We found a 50 × 100 foot lot in a somewhat tattered part of Santa Monica. Working on a minimal budget, the four of us undertook all the demolition and construction to make a livable building of the "tear-down."

We gutted the inside, whose 575 square feet had been divided into six tiny rooms. The total scope of the work was like slipping a new drawer into an old bureau.

In planning the house, we addressed the questions of priority in how we live. There is an effort to balance dynamic spaces with quiet spaces so that parts of the house can be serene, and others active.

For us the pleasure of the exercise lay in changing a shack into a small world that lends itself equally to being a quiet personal retreat or a lively social place.

Buzz Yudell and Tina Beebe

LIST OF PARTICULARS

Yudell-Beebe house
Location: Santa Monica, California
Architects and Designers:
Buzz Yudell, Tina Beebe, and
John Ruble
Budget: $15,000, renovation
$40,000, house and land
Nominal space: 570 square feet
Perceived space: 720 square feet

insertion of an aesthetic non sequitur within the context of the prosaic outline created an essential hierarchy that ordered the entire project. The oblong space effectively penetrates the existing front wall to create an entry. In addition, the creation of an internally focused space gives a sense of *porché,* or carved excision of space from mass. The implementation of a void amid spatial in-fill within such a small context creates a dialogue between form and space of subtle ramifications.

This positive void serves as the link between and the delineator of the cooking, sleeping, and bathing spaces left over after its spatial form manifests itself. It is, in effect, a cornerless heart for the home. Such an unexpected space relieves the fear of encountering small boxes of space set into the small box of a house form.

Obviously problems are created when such an eccentric element is imposed on a simple (and diminutive) plan. The sense of occupying an empty swimming pool is relieved when over half the actual wall surface area of the elliptic space is removed. The remnant parts include a simple cornice providing a definition of the corner dining area and a framed passage to the sleeping area. Finally, the vestigial wall remnants frame three large-scale openings to the sleeping area, which in turn become marvelously integrated seating and sleeping bays.

The curvilinear imposition is overtly contrapuntal to the inert orthogonal box, but more than cheap-thrills dissonance, this lyric insertion engenders a sense of spatial and formal ambiguity reinforced by its crucial posture amid all the spaces. It serves as both a divider and a link. It is at once a solid shape and a transparent

1

All photos by Tim Street Porter

Figure 1   *Entry. A cascade of elliptic influence. Custom fenestration adds a depth of detailing enriching the curvilinear interface with a blank-box house form. Note the ordered light fixtures above and the ebullient use of pots.*

Figure 2   *Interior. Entry (right) responds to curving influence with a glazed release. Seating is inserted into the interstitial space between existing rectilinear perimeter and new elliptic space. The sleeping area (left) nestles behind the wall, while its extension provides more seating. Integrated elements such as these maximize spatial efficiency while creating a sense of thorough design. Tina Beebe's surface treatments reinforce the latent meanings of the forms imposed. Color, texture, and materials interface to engender a sense of quietly kinetic happenstance. Note the skylight above the central excised bay. Note also the main carrying beam above.*

Figure 3   *Plan. The skewed ellipse violates all rectilinear influences of the existing perimeter. The powerful imposition effectively reels in the bookcase wall (top center) and creates seating within the interstitial space between existing wall and new space (right). Note the imposed column (center), which collects roof loads.*

2

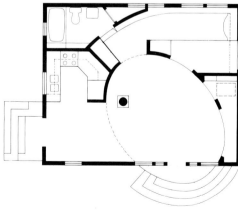

Floor Plan

4

All drawings by the architects

organizing influence. The power of its imposed application is both diffused and enhanced as articulated by Yudell, Beebe, and Ruble.

A simple idea need not be simplistically expressed. In small houses the imposition of a crudely applied large-scale element is disaster unmitigated. The designers realized that possibility and took the notion of an imposed large-scale counterpoint and refined its influence.

Without a skillful redress of the remnant spaces, and their re-creation as closely scrutinized and thoroughly designed subdivisions of distilled functional density, the curving imposition would be an awkward inconvenience. However, when available space is coalesced to form a large-scale core of void in a small house, the expected pinch of compromise is avoided. The need to condense the ancillary spaces, because of the dominant ellipsoid imposition, engenders inventiveness and insight. The depth of the design is made possible by the limits imposed on the designers.

Whether there is a constructed reality in the form of four walls or there is an equally tangible limit on the money to be spent, a small-house design can create enhanced delight and utility because of, not just in spite of, its defined boundaries. Limits can indeed be liberating, and it is in the release of constriction, conceptually as well as physically, that small houses can afford a unique opportunity for architectural expression.

4

5

Figure 4 *Corner kitchen. This extremely compact kitchen, with the oven as its focal point, is both thoroughly informal and densely packed with storage space. Note the refrigerator to far right with cabinet above.*

Figure 5 *Sleeping-den-living interface. As elements collide, space, texture, form, and light all dance in a carefully choreographed interaction.*

Figure 6 *Axonometric. This roofless view inside gives the best indication of how a simple perimeter is given life via a large-scale imposition. Note the application of new custom windows and doors to both create an entry and facilitate a release of the power of the applied elliptic room geometry. Note how the ancillary spatial subdivisions are as densely packed as the new void is open. The custom fenestration, the curving bookcases, entry steps, and column are unexpected elements that are either effected by, defined by, or enclosed within the new grand element.*

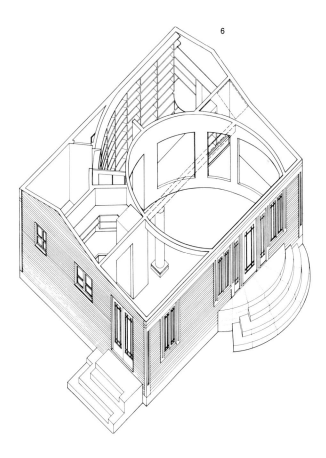

6

Creative Construction

A simple shell houses a small fantasy of ascending parts, enlivened space, and divided activities.

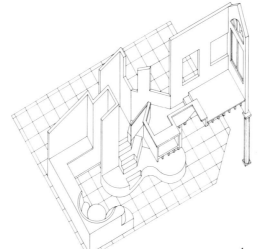

An artist was confronted with a twin problem: where to live and where to work in the crowded bustle of Los Angeles. A tiny building lot became available surrounded on two sides by macadam, cars, and industrial buildings. The other two sides addressed a residential neighborhood.

The young artist seized upon the site as a symbolic solution to her dual dilemma. The creative process need not be held at arm's length and visited during office hours only, even if an ancient printing press and massive type cases are necessary for the creative spark to manifest itself.

Having resolved the internal quandary of dual accommodation under one roof, the young artist brought her newfound site and focus to the nearby architectural firm of Moore Ruble Yudell.

The architects were equally enthusiastic about the prospect of creating a symbiotic combination of spaces. The cliché "Art is my life" may evoke a sense of extraordinary devotion and singularity of purpose, but when one's domicile is intended to embrace one's profession as well as the space in which to eat, sleep, and bathe, complications arise. These complicated programmatic inputs were made even more problematic by a ridiculously low budget for building.

Just as art flourishes amid adversity, somehow the pinched site, squeezed budget, and overloaded design program have conspired to release the very best of architectural energies as applied to the small-house form.

Wedged into a corner of a back lot, the site did not allow for any plan configuration save one conforming to the regulating site boundaries imposed upon it, that is, a simple rectangle. Obviously, tight budgets must provide enclosure no mat-

ARCHITECT'S STATEMENT

The studio sits behind an existing small house with a commercial parking lot to the south and east and a residential neighborhood to the north and west. Its wood frame and stucco construction are consistent with the front house, a modest Los Angeles bungalow of the 1920s, as well as with the rest of the neighborhood.

For us and the artist, the studio is exciting for its economical making of a modest, carefully composed shell and for its integration of a work space with tiny living spaces choreographed for the pleasures of moving and entertaining. Living and working are separated in a manner that avoids intrusion but allows each a voyeuristic sense of the excitement of the other.

Buzz Yudell

LIST OF PARTICULARS

Artist's studio
Location: Los Angeles, California
Architects: Moore Ruble Yudell
Budget: $40,000
Nominal space: 850 square feet
Perceived space: 1200 square feet

ter how tight they are, and Moore Ruble Yudell—in the form of Buzz Yudell and John Ruble—looked to the essentials of the simple (and yet potentially overloaded) programmatic design requirements to form their conception of the house-cum-studio.

Any house must provide space for preparing food, for dining, for taking care of personal hygiene, and for sleeping. The only additional space that must be addressed by any architect is that needed for other activities—social, professional, or personal. It is that space which reflects the idiosyncratic nature of the client more than any other. In this case, an artist's home had to provide space to create and implement her art as a printer. The process is messy and space-consumptive, and it demands long hours of focused labor.

A hot spot of daily focus must have its spatial antithesis. Unrelenting focus distorts perspective and dulls creativity. Without rest and reflection, activity loses meaning. Every home has one spot where literal re-creation is allowed to happen without the outside world intruding. The bedroom is an intimate recharging battery for hearts, minds, and bodies. If it is set amid the chaos of work, its ability to provide rest and perspective is greatly compromised, if not made impossible.

So Ruble and Yudell seized upon the mandatory distinction between work space and sleep space to effect their building's essential organization. Given the limited space upon which to build, the only way to provide meaningful separation was by lofting the sleeping area into a second story.

The opportunity to create an externally focused space of intimate proportions was not missed by the architects. The

Figure 1 *Interior. Presses (right), stair (center), kitchen-dining area (left), and structure (upper left) are woven together by a simple system of walls. Integrated seating, skylights, steps, and bookcases all further mesh the elements employed.*

Figure 2 *Loft. Stairs (left) wind to the singular solitude of the sleeping loft (upper right). Divisions are facilitated by seating, balconies, and levels. Note the beckoning fan window and the open glazing below.*

Figure 3 *A tower unapologetic. Fairly dominating the mini-piazza below, a simplified tower keys entry and provides focus.*

All photos by Tim Street Porter

1

2

3

Figure 4 *Seating. Part sculpture, part softening counterpart to the simple starkness of a small house, this element is both focal point and mediator.*

Figure 5 *Axonometric with exterior envelope removed.*

Figure 6 *Plan. Angles, curves, and level changes create a large-scale subsystem of inserted elements within the context of a simple plan footprint. Printing (lower left), entry (upper left), stair (center), dining area (upper right), and wet core of kitchen and bath (lower right) are all linked and divided by the internal construction.*

4

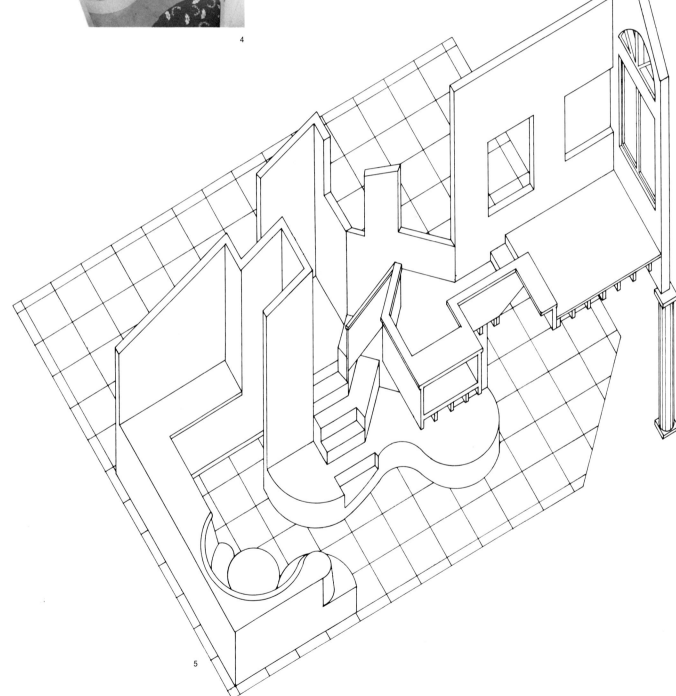

5

All drawings by the architect

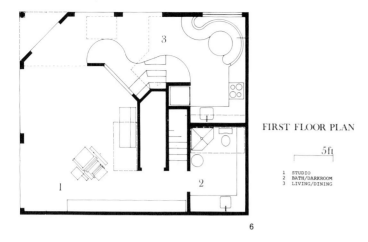

FIRST FLOOR PLAN

___5ft

1 STUDIO
2 BATH/DARKROOM
3 LIVING/DINING

6

bedroom became simply a platform upon which to sleep, surrounded on three sides by natural light. A reinforcement of its identity as a singularly special place in the house was effected by the elevation of its interior space and exterior form to create a gable-faced tower.

From this essential divination of function and form, an entire house seems to be generated. Externally this lofted tower had to be embraced by the much larger horizontal mass of the house. A simple double-pitched roof (two intersecting sheds forming a single hip) has its form oriented in support of, and deference to, the bedroom.

Internally, the lofty perch of the bedroom necessitated access. A standard solution might simply allow a stair to stand aside and let people up while letting the art-activity-dominated space run rampant below. Such a standard, passive solution does not address the need for functional distinction and is, in truth, boring. Instead the architects saw the stair as a vertical line that could provide both spatial separation and internal formal focus. A stair may indeed simply let us get elevated, but in this case the stair is itself a meandering event, a defining articulated object coursing through the relatively large studio space defining a boundary between art and life.

A secondary ordering motif was used. The only subdivisions present in any undivided rectangle are the spaces defined at the corners by the simple linear interface of the exterior walls. As said, the bedroom claimed a proud second-story corner, but this small house's other specialized spaces of entry, kitchen, and bath were allocated in corner postures as well, helping to provide an order to the first floor.

Entry occurs at the corner above which hovers the bedroom tower. The door is pulled back as a chamfered plane, leaving the corner supported by a column.

The implicit result of this angled entry is a diagonal axis. The stair imposition responds to this as the internal formal pyrotechnics begin. Suffice it to say that playful curves, jogged diagonals, and multiple level changes combine with isolated subspaces for dressing, writing, and sitting to create a kinetic sculpture of architectural events. Perforations are effected and stair undersides exposed to allow visual penetration between the eating-cooking corner and the studio corner dominating the west half of the house.

The level of architectural articulation and expression in this 25 × 30 foot building is rare and inspiring. Functions are held distinct by the stair imposition and corner orientation, but simultaneously they are connected visually by the consistently inconsistent form of the stair.

Above all this ascending activity, a placid roof of exposed framing and appropriately placed skylights provides the gentle affirmation of abiding enclosure. The consistent objectification of stairs, walls, seating, storage bins for the printing press, type, and work benches is allowed by the free flow of space around and about the entire house. This flow also provides visual links that serve to defeat the sense of limits one might normally find in an 850-square-foot house.

It took 3 years for the finish to be applied to the house staked out by the architects. The time spent by the owner considering and effecting the details applied enriches the entire project.

Obviously, children are not accommodated here, nor is energy efficiency a major design influence. But these mitigating reductions in programmatic input are more than compensated for in the house's response to the challenge of providing a work space.

Successful buildings begin simply, then wax complicated, only to finally reveal simplicity again. Buzz Yudell and John Ruble turned a tiny house into a sophisticated juxtaposition of form, space, and interior articulation, without violating domestic scale or complicating the design to the point of absurdity.

Integrated Idiosyncrasy

William Lipsey designs, builds, and generally applies himself to his own house.

T he rough-hewn gentility of rural Colorado has evoked romanticization in song, exposure in the media, and exploitation by architects as a foil for some fairly slick residential designs. These High Tech homes are technogically integrated to accommodate every environmental exigency but have little or nothing to do with the existing social surroundings (their designs are somewhat akin to putting home computers in chicken coops). These hyperattenuated architectural conceits tend to touch the landscape with the sensitivity of space capsules.

William Lipsey lives among the architectural mood swings of Aspen. Seeing the conflict inherent in the aesthetic apartheid of a High Tech style so high that it is somewhat out of control and a Sub-bourgeois Bucolic style, Lipsey divined his own aesthetic integration of the best of both worlds.

The distended mansions evidencing aesthetic counterpoint (if not contempt) for their surroundings were indeed energy-efficient, although their owners were not in an income bracket to appreciate the savings on much more than a conceptual level. The rambling shacks that dotted the landscape were indeed scaled to humanity and were constructed of commonsense materials, although these buildings were intended primarily to shed rain and snow from miners' heads—with little or no attention to aesthetics. So one architecture for the elite and one for the masses existed in Colorado in mutual exclusivity until William Lipsey and a few other architects began to give prosaic architecture aesthetic insight and technological depth.

At times called Victorian High Tech, this is an architecture of the loose-fit

---

ARCHITECT'S STATEMENT

Designing a house for oneself is really difficult. Whereas clients usually have a very limited number of styles they like, architects designing for themselves have to come to grips with a myriad of options.

I narrowed the options early on by sticking to an Early Ranch vernacular palette:

- Board-and-batt siding
- Double-hung windows
- Corrugated metal roofing

The morphology of this house shares something of the spirit and romance of those tall, lonely, anonymous farmhouses one sees in the distance from the interstate.

William Lipsey

LIST OF PARTICULARS

Lipsey house
Location: Aspen, Colorado
Architect: William Lipsey
Budget: Unavailable
Nominal space: 1200 square feet
Perceived space: 1500 square feet

---

detail, of a seemingly retroactive history, and an implicitly ad hoc sense of gratuitous juxtaposition. Of course, preconceived innocence is quite a sophisticated art, and the danger is that stage-set hyperbole can create a sense of stressed credibility. But this house has a life of its own and a sense of itself that one has to suspect are the direct results of Bill Lipsey's posture as an architect, client, and builder.

The single pristine datum of this multipiece composition is the cubic formal mass upon which all of the parts are applied. Gable roof, shed-roofed lean-to additions, saddlebag addendums, shed dormers, bay windows, awnings, flower boxes, a deck, and an occasional window all prance about the cubic root, generally respecting centers but occasionally without an organizing orientation.

All of this activity, plus some essential planning of axes and spatial hierarchies, is intended to engender a sense of delightful informality, of a domestic architecture with down-home roots. There is no metaphoric symbolism here, only contextual allusion. The materials employed—board-and-batten siding, corrugated steel roof, and rustic trim—reinforce the rural character.

The reader should realize that all of these applications, allusions, and kinetic permutations occur within the context of a 1200-square-foot house. In terms of perceptual extension of a home's impact, few projects can match the success of this modest one.

A tripartite plan division skillfully uses the space afforded by the seemingly gratuitous application of the formal extensions described. The ground floor accommodates two bedrooms, an exquisitely

Figure 1 *Southwest and entry. Applications of lean-to shed, solar generator (set over utility area and mudroom), porch, and ascendant shed dormer all expand and diffuse the potentially stark gable house form. Note the considered centrality of the south elevation and the decorative eave stepping.*

Figure 2 *Living room. Facing south, the owner-fabricated stair hangs in stringy counterpoint to the rather prosaic space effected. Thoroughly contemporary furnishings add spice with their quiet dissonance amid a farmhouse ambience. Note that the pressed-tin ceiling, rough-hewn floor, and shag rug provide textural variety to the simple space.*

Figure 3 *Wood stove and bay window.*

All photos by Gordon H. Schenck, Jr.

1

2   3

4

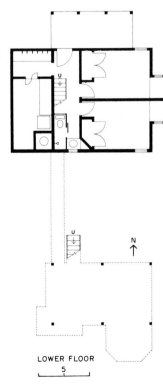

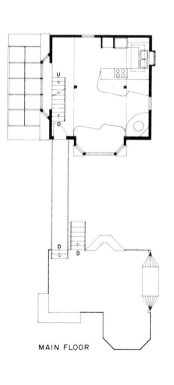

5

LOWER FLOOR

5

MAIN FLOOR

UPPER FLOOR

N

U

Courtesy of *Architectural Record*

modest bath, a mudroom, and a utility space. The second floor is an open-platform, *piano-nobile* living, cooking, and eating space. The third floor, its available space necked down by the intrusion of the gable roof form, is given over to a modest master bedroom suite.

Continuous through this plan evolution is a southerly slot of circulation space, which serves as a convection space as well. The tight interior spaces are given life by the zesty application of proasic domestic materials.

Ornamental pressed-tin ceiling panelling, rough pine flooring, an occasional antique appliance are counter-pointed by some overtly modern lighting fixtures and stringy-steel stair detailing.

Structurally, the central support of the house is of post-and-beam construction, while the perimeter is of standard 2 × 4 framing.

A simple form, standard building technology, and a host of applied elements defer to one overt organizing influence—solar orientation. The fundamental utility of this now-programmatic organizational technology is very much at home with the extremely informal ambience of the building.

The small size of this home plays a crucial role in reducing the potential for visual chaos. Without an abidingly tight perimeter, the applications would form the rambling arrays of agglommerated addendums that represent the downside of traditional rural domesticity.

Bill Lipsey captures life without creating a sense of an architectural zoo. The lively intercourse between all the standard pieces and parts so densely juxtaposed gains integrity by the orientations of those pieces and parts and by the building's unflagging commitment to solar gain. Crucial to the success of so much activity is the restraint imposed by the home's tiny size.

The Lipsey house conveys the value of considered spatial reduction that results in energy efficiencies and aesthetic clarification. It's a happy consequence that such amenities are in addition to those basic economies effected from the construction of a small house.

William Lipsey has the opportunity to realize both these tangible efficiencies and visceral gratifications on a daily basis.

6

Figure 4 *Southwest view.*

Figure 5 *Plans. Three floors, three identities linked by the southerly convection-circulation space. On entry, one encounters a naked stair bypassing the bedrooms (right) and the service spaces used as heat-generating solar spaces. Note the distinct sink, which allows for an extremely efficient bath layout. The second level presents a* piano-nobile *public area with northerly corners defining kitchen and wood stove, while south and east bays afford exposure to view and spatial release and focus. Note the remote deck accessed across a long bridge. Top floor is an extended rectangle sitting beneath a double-shed dormer, housing a master bedroom suite.*

Figure 6 *East. As seen from the remote deck, this proud facade addresses a beautiful view and orients the deck dweller toward home. Note the absolutely generic quality of all the elements employed; the sense of life is derived solely from the considered orientation of the parts applied and the juxtaposition of the various formal components developed by the architect.*

Setting Sail

Turner Brooks launches a small house.

S et amid the rolling hills of Vermont, a proud object maintains its dignity despite its relatively diminutive presence in the landscape.

Designed by architect Turner Brooks, this house has the charm of a considered enigma. A large-scale roof form, an attenuated gable, is unbowed in its dynamic natural setting. Yet the house itself barely exceeds 1000 square feet. The predominant architectural organizer, formal symmetry, creates a centered, composed, and rational face to the world, and yet one wing is discernibly bent in a vaguely rakish manner. The preeminent roof form, seemingly all-encompassing, is revealed to be only a partial covering for the house. Brooks applied a rear appendage to his simple, expressive roof in the form of a lean-to wing.

The windows, doors, and siding reveal a precisely calculated combination of traditional surfaces and components, and yet the central focus of the front facade is a large-scale array of four large windows that is anything but subtle in its detailing or impact.

Similarly, all the detailing of eaves, mouldings, and siding is thoroughly standard and conveys a timeless carpenter's approach to the craft of construction. However, the two most isolated elements of the house, the porch columns, are detailed to become caricaturish abstractions.

With a consistent inconsistency, Brooks brings the simplest of forms to life. Where antiquity left such ad hoc variety up to the personalizing touches of a succession of owners, Brooks short-circuits the aesthetic life cycle of a home to enrich his simple house form in the here and now. In this way Brooks avoided the temptation to apply styles to effect aes-

---

ARCHITECT'S STATEMENT

On the north side of this house the low, sloping roofs pull it down and anchor it to the hill. On the south it lifts and, led by its staunch columns and bay window, sails out into the landscape. The long expanse of the gable is snapped together by the taut stretch of the porch roof below. The heavy columns anchor and somehow exaggerate this stretch. They scale up this little house (somewhat as the giant-scale trim work scales up the tiny old Greek Revival houses in the area), and they make this humble little house confront successfully the large landscape rolling away below it to the south.

The house is simple in plan. A central cast-iron stove with a stair winding up behind it, a bay window pushing out in front toward the south, and in the back, lined up on this axis, the master bed. The living room to the west and the kitchen and entrance area to the east are wings stretching out from this center. Standing centered in the house with your back to the stove and stair, facing into the bay, with the landscape away before you, a wing on each side of you, one feels magnificently in control of the destiny of this house as it cruises out into the landscape.

Turner Brooks

LIST OF PARTICULARS

Hurd house

Location: Rural Vermont

Architect: Turner Brooks

Budget: Not available

Nominal space: 1000 square feet

Perceived space: 1100 square feet

---

thetic postures in an effort to veil the latent innocent dignity of a small rural home.

Turner Brooks can articulate so many aesthetic permutations on such a small subject simply because he has rigorously addressed the essential aspect of all successful small-house designs—the fundamental formal expression of the house's shape. Deriving the form of the house from local farm buildings, nautical images, and a personal sense of scale and aesthetic kinetics, the architect has succeeded in creating an architectural event both potent and sweet.

The interior of this expressive volume is starkly distilled for maximum efficiency, allowing four people to inhabit a tiny house with a minimum of compromise. However, accommodating a family within the confines of 1000 feet is not without *any* compromise.

Two children sleep in one bedroom. There is one bathroom on the first floor. There is no spatial definition between areas for any social function. There is no basement. There are very few closets. The stair is both tight and winding.

However, there are also interior amenities that belie the inherent constriction of such a tight house envelope. Two small double-height spaces allow for solar-heated air to convect into the second floor. The master bedroom is a semidetached wing with light and air on three sides. Interior windows connect spaces. The kitchen is relatively generous in size. The front porch is of a grand scale, and the size of the windows is extraordinarily large for the spaces they are oriented to. The house is a model of passive solar site orientation and design principles.

These elements enhanced and diminished are merely the tangible results of

Paul Ferrino

Figure 1 *Context. A classic house form is dwarfed by and yet controls a lush Vermont hillside.*

2

Photos on this page by Turner Brooks

3

Figure 2 *The front, south. Pride manifest in innocent ascendance, this frontally posturing gable is both rustic and subtle. Note the overt ganging of stock windows, creating a slightly exaggerated sense of scaled differentiation. Note also the broad expanse of wall, animated by a variety of cedar siding types, allowing the multiple windows to coexist. Note last the quiet asymmetry beneath the left side of the porch, as a side wall is bent, creating an angled shadow amid the order.*

Figure 3 *Angled prospect. The caricaturish columns support a broad porch overhang, beneath which sits a large central bay. Note the three siding types in the gable pediment, and the additional siding types used to articulate other subordinate building elements.*

Figure 4 *Back of the house. The proud frontality of the gable face obscures some less formal elements applied to the back of the house. Note that the major lean-to is the master bedroom.*

Figure 5 *Plans. A narrow bay has a bedroom, a porch, and a bathroom applied to its back. The front of the home presents a large deck to the southern view, while the second floor rests below the peaked roof, allowing a two-bed bedroom flanked by low storage rooms. Note the two convection spaces flanking the bedroom as well.*

4

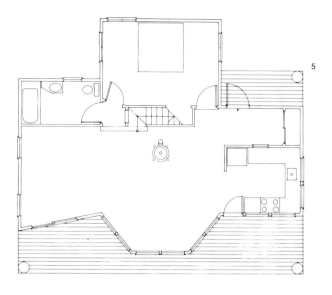

5

FIRST FLOOR

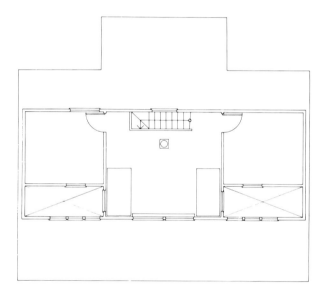

SECOND FLOOR

Drawings by the architect

extraordinary soul-searching by both the architect and his clients. Creativity cannot manifest a good fit between owner, house, and site without rigorous application of observed fact and prioritized design criteria no matter what the size of the house.

Turner Brooks has taken a site of sweeping hills and dominated it with a tiny house. Because an ultimately purposeful construction has been set within a rambling context, the isolated focus of the home can create a singular datum from which to measure the landscape.

It is precisely the measure of a house's latent identity that can elevate a small house into the realm of artistic expression. By an egocentric miscalculation, a mini-monster can be born. By the surrender to mediocrity (by way of fear), a small house can become an ongoing apologetic rationalization. Brooks has avoided both extremes by an unrelenting application of detached perspective and focused creative ability.

Eloquent Locomotion

A small house cruises into our hearts and minds.

Turner Brooks is not vague about his design intentions. As his statement (right) indicates, Brooks applies kinetic aesthetics to static structures. This may seem inherently contradictory, and the notion of the form of a house being imitative of motion conjures up images of summer-stock stage sets. But the results of this architect's efforts at perambulatory posturing are positively inspirational as evidenced in this extraordinary house.

This is a building of three parts, all in interaction, but all distinctly self-empowered.

A central tower house is flanked by two expressive wings. The middle portion of the building is a three-story construction containing the entry, a bath, the master bedroom, and a loft. On one side of this simple form derived from a square plan is the living wing. The kitchen, dining room, and living room are housed beneath a swooping beveled roof. An open plan gains spatial impact by the use of a cathedralized ceiling supported by a huge exposed wood-frame truss and a single-step level change. The last element in this tripartite composition is the most unforgettably suggestive. Never were a stair, a bath, and a bedroom so sweetly embraced by a house form. The last wing described is simply a semiparabolic roof form extending from the ground to the loft level. The formal simplicity belies the visceral impact. Images of a billowing sail, a paddle wheel, a churning thresher, or locomotive wheels are latently expressed in this "butt end."

No matter what specific identity is evoked in the massing, all images convey the general quality of vibrant kinesthesis Brooks has endeavored to engender. The vertical tower, laterally expansive living wing, and curvaceous end wing all seem to dance to the same tune under Brooks's influence. All these various components can be monstrous in the context of some bloated architectural collision. Conversely, the varietal nature of a "poly-personality" construction can result in a confused jumble of pieces and parts when the house created is 1200-square-feet small. How does Brooks avoid these pitfalls?

At the risk of oversimplification, one could say that Brooks applies a sensitive perspective and an artful sense of expressive detailing to create a cogent house out of disparate parts. Legitimizing these thoughts are the results depicted in the photographs. While all three parts have discontinuous roofs—one a curve, one a gable, the other a beveling blanket—the siding, trim, and house perimeter are thoroughly integrated between Brooks's triple play.

Openings in the form are exquisitely expressive and semiabstracted. Either these windows are in coordinated linkage with a wrapping molding datum, or they stand in sublime counterpoint to the band's continuity. Within this simple division, windows express themselves as either centers, progressions, or ad hoc perforations of the clapboard wrap. Corners tend to attract windows, as do gable center lines. Even other windows tend to attract windows, creating clusters of fenestration, while leaving relatively large expanses of clapboard siding uninterrupted.

By expressing a variety of consistent rules of surface treatment to bind the basic building parts together, Brooks both orchestrates the formal activity and further articulates some of the components' latent properties.

This mesh of elemental expression and formal integration has its counterpart in

---

ARCHITECT'S STATEMENT

I have done night drawings of this house in charcoal in which it is seen sliding through a smoldering dark landscape. I see my houses as objects in the landscape, taut and somewhat streamlined, moving along under their own power. They are not relaxed and spread out over the landscape like the old farm buildings that create their own human-made landscape without buildings, fields, fences, etc. Rather they are plunked down on the edge of some abandoned meadowland and must make their own way through the landscape. Their shapes are nostalgic to me. They remind me of my parents' first car, a 1949 Ford, which I found both dignified and voluptuous. But it is more than this. In all my houses there are places where you feel that you are in total command of the house. Those spaces are analogous to the bridge of a ship, the control center of a locomotive, etc. In these crucial spaces one feels connected to the entire house; one has comprehended the whole and has, in a sense, merged with it so that it has become an extension of one's body. You are at its brain center, at the helm. There is the satisfying feeling that you are steering this large object through the landscape.

Turner Brooks

LIST OF PARTICULARS

McClane house

Location: Starksboro, Vermont

Architect: Turner Brooks

Budget: Not available

Nominal space: 1200 square feet

Perceived space: 1600 square feet

1

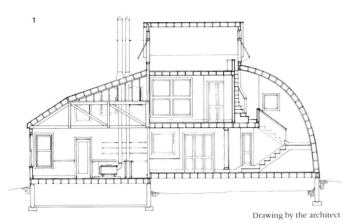

Drawing by the architect

Figure 1 *Section. The three formal elements evidence themselves in this section. Living area (left), tower (center), and stair (right) display their differentiated roof forms and spatial qualities.*

Figure 2 *A study in multiple identities melded in motion. Curved, peaked, and beveled roofs are bound together with a continuous perimeter and homogenous surface treatment.*

2

3

Turner Brooks

Turner Brooks

4

Cervin Robinson

Figure 3 *A billowing prow collected by a triumphantly gabled wheelhouse. Lurking lower left is the third component, the laterally extended living wing in the form of a single-story bay.*

Figure 4 *The living room. Windows dance, walls bend, discrete parts announce themselves in a sea of space. The dominant aspect amid all these pyrotechnics is the entry axis (center). A singular, abstractly organizing linearity can give chaos a backbone.*

Figure 5 *Entry axis. This axis is received by the window beyond, and the horizontal focus is rewarded by the beckoning living space beyond. Note the implicit dialogue between the antique door (left) and column (right), helping to define entry.*

Figure 6 *Master bedroom overlook. In a position of secondary power to the crowning loft, this interior window reels in the "marching" windows and presents a varied vista of space, surface, and light.*

5

the internal workings of the house. A singular visual and circulatory axis connects all three building parts, focused on the stair at the bulbous end and a window at the prismatic living room end, with the entry oriented amidships. The central tower is linked to the extreme wings via the stair in the rounded end and interior windows in the living end. The climactic loft overlooks both roofscapes.

The variety of spaces enclosed by the expressive envelope is mind-boggling given the simple two-bedroom, two-bath, 1200-square-foot program accommodated.

The ambiguously expansive living-wing space extends from the standard flat slabs of space of the central tower's first two floors. The extreme linearity of the linking axis is received by the arching underside of the stair wing's roof. Atop all this activity sits the tight cathedral of space of the tower loft.

All of these sophisticated spatial and formal interactions are articulated with the simplest of materials, detailing, and components. The innocence of the mediums employed is in perfect harmony with the house setting, the bucolic hills of Vermont.

It is the essential dialogue between house and site that has generated Brooks's vision of domestic accommodation. Vermont has a gentle ruggedness reminiscent of the sea. The nautical allusions of this house are unmistakable. A diminutive juggernaut, a purposeful tug, a proud paddle wheeler, this house fairly plows the landscape. The loft as wheelhouse, the living room wing as bow, the stair stern as engine room, all the constituent parts are manipulated by Brooks so that they act in overtly allusive concert.

Whether naval or simply mobile in intention, the results are unforgettable and somehow timeless. Turner Brooks has crafted a surprisingly effervescent home of rather prosaic parts. Given the limitations of the house program and the power of the building's situation, this architect has created a quietly dominant home of immense allure and positive power.

Cervin Robinson

6

A Lookout to the Landscape

In rural Connecticut, Roderic Hartung creates a variegated vision of country living.

Fifteen years ago, Rod Hartung was an architect based in New York City. In his possession was a 15-acre parcel of land in Old Lyme, Connecticut. Such was the power of this site that Hartung saw the preservation of the natural elements as his fundamental orientation for the design of a rural retreat.

A house has a footprint on the earth, and environmental intrusion is reduced as this footprint is diminished in area. A house is built to serve its occupants as well as respect its site, and the only way to accommodate human life while minimizing natural disruption is via the vertical stacking of space.

There are several correlative benefits to the use of the vertical dimension. First, an array of visual prospects rising above the natural visual din at ground level is presented as the occupant ascends through the house. Second, passive solar heating and natural cooling are assisted by a vertical organization. Solar-heated air is naturally recirculated via convection during winter and vented via a vertical flue during summer. Last, amid the tall growth of mature trees, a vertical house form sympathizes with its natural neighbors and beckons those approaching.

Hartung's design has several ordering attitudes that enable a high degree of formal and spatial articulation without perceptual overload.

The first ordering system is the 6-inch shingling module. All window, eave, and exterior wall heights conform to the lines formed by the consistent shingle coursing. It is important to note that almost all glazing is custom-fabricated to facilitate this perfect fit.

The second ordering element is the vertical datum of chimney, stair, and util-ity chase that serves as tree trunk to the branching forms and spaces. Often referred to in aesthetic lingo as a "spine," this functional hub gains enormous perceptual impact by the use of unencumbered space between the elements it orients. Without the presence of enough space and light, a simple vertical organization would be spiritually mute. Hartung has given this architectural fulcrum power by creating a sense, both externally and internally, that all elements of the house are spawned by and oriented to this singular constant. An interesting consequence of the ascendant axis is the presence of a second major horizontal axis encountered upon entry. The dynamic interface of two powerful functional and aesthetic lines of action belies the actual size of the house.

With a hierarchical dominance ensured by consistent formal, functional, and spatial deference to the central core and shingle course module, a great deal of expression can be realized without visual confusion or dissipating detail.

The highly successful articulation of virtually all the components presented by the house was helped by the status of Hartung as both owner and client and by a protracted period of design stretching into several years. In fact the final phase of the entire design and construction process is the occupancy by Hartung of the house as a principal residence rather than a part-time vacation home.

By the architect's recognition and reinforcement of the variety of elements that constitute a house—both functionally and aesthetically—this small house is made rich. By the architect's recognition and reinforcement of the vertical axis—both functionally and aesthetically—this tall house is made to work.

ARCHITECT'S STATEMENT

The house is tall and thin, rising over the surrounding oak trees. This makes it easier to cool and heat the house with passive techniques. On the north facade, a windowless wall curves to the protected front entry, shunning cold winter winds. Floor-to-ceiling windows on the southwest side take advantage of the prevailing summer breezes, a natural cooling system. Easterly skylights are protected by summer foliage, yet effectively warm the house in winter. Acting not only as part of the energy system, the heating ducts, with the highest acting as a warm-air return, function as design elements, visually connecting the vertical planes of the house.

Roderic Hartung

LIST OF PARTICULARS

Hartung house
Location: Old Lyme, Connecticut
Architect: Roderic Hartung, AIA
Budget: $70,000 (1976)
Nominal space: 1280 square feet
Perceptual space: 1770 square feet

Rod Hartung   1

Rod Hartung   2   3   Stanley C. Lichens

Figure 1 *North view, seen upon imminent entry. Five distinct identities are presented, despite the paucity of glazing due to a lack of potential solar gain. Central is the masonry mass fireplace, keying the internal vertical axis. Flanking are the chamfered living room (right) and curving study (left). Tucked to the left, a low quarter-round wall keys entry, while above it all, the lofty studio respects only the chimney's height. Note how all roof-pitch points, eaves, glazing, and overhanging lines are keyed to the 6-inch shingle course module.*

Figure 2 *Entry. The encountered half-round study wall (right) wraps into a protected entry portal nestled beneath a double-cantilevered overhang. The entry axis fairly glows from within with south light. Again the shingle coursing dominates all formal manipulations.*

Figure 3 *South. A levitated shingle construction faces the sun. The formal float is achieved via slight cantilevering of the first floor beyond the foundation edge. Note the double-course shingled datum (left center) above the simple deck. The corner location of the deck allows its space to be perceived from both the kitchen (center) and the living room (left). Note how all windows are custom-fabricated, allowing a perfect mesh with the ever-wrapping shingling courses.*

4   Rod Hartung

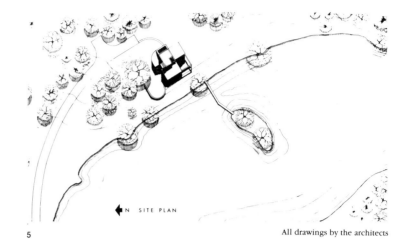

N SITE PLAN

5   All drawings by the architects

6

Jeremy Dodd

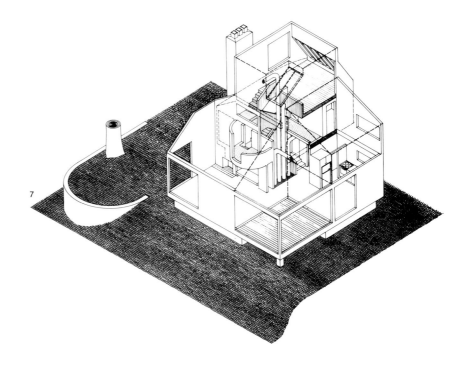

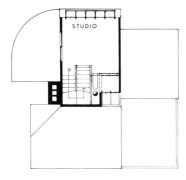

TOP LEVEL

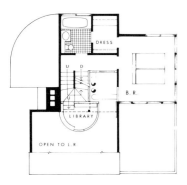

UPPER LEVEL

LOWER LEVEL

8

Figure 4 *Entry indicator. A lyric element, this shingle whimsy rainbows toward the door. Radial butt joints and curved course lines display a care and craftsmanship extraordinary in exterior detailing. Note how all lines derive from the wall to the left. An unsettling curved cantilever beyond allows the study to fairly hover above the ground cover.*

Figure 5 *Site plan. A long curving drive allows a turning presentation of the house as the approach is made. Note how the deck orients one to a view of the small island to the right.*

Figure 6 *Living room. Typical open-corner custom glazing allows the view over the pond to dominate the room. Note the looming library cantilever at upper right.*

Figure 7 *Axonometric. With roof and bedroom floor eliminated (roof outline is indicated with dashed lines), the various levels are presented. Note the bull-nose library balcony at living room center. Note also the deck at the bottom of the sketch, defined by the extended plate lines of the flanking walls.*

Figure 8 *Plans. Spaces pirouette about the central stair. Note the implicit cross axis of the stair itself, the heat ducts, and the kitchen window. Note how one corner in each room receives double glazing. The central stair serves to separate spaces horizontally while providing linkage vertically. Each upper floor serves a single function—as bedroom or studio, respectively.*

Figure 9 *Entry axis. Note the powerful intersection of the vertical core (right) and the uninhibited prospect of the living room (left). Stair, space, and ducts weave in seductive, upwardly mobile interplay. Note the use of tongue-and-groove surfaces for the stair and ceiling above, delineating a subsystem from the predominant painted gypsum-board walls surrounding the axis. Unapologetically cantilevered beam ends (top) and distributing ducts (flawlessly enameled) reinforce the latent kinetics.*

Figure 10 *Vertical axis. Ducts, rails, plants, lights, and walls ascend amid space and light. The interplay aspires to the south light with an unmistakable positive sensibility.*

Figure 11 *View down. This is Modernist vision of bypassing systems, voids, planes, and space. Note the sliding clerestory room divider (top). Note also the broad-board bedroom floor pattern set opposite to the hallway below.*

Figure 12 *Duct detail. Providing an aesthetic reinforcement of the perforation of the monolithic floor by the sinuous duct, this seminautical detail conveys a depth of thought greatly enhancing to any small-house design.*

10

Photos 9–12 by Rod Hartung

11

12

Unassuming High Tech

Richard Fernau and Laura Hartman conspire to swaddle a thoroughly engineered house in familiar clothing.

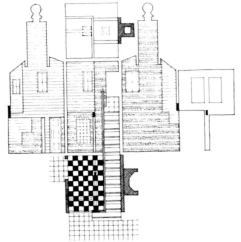

Central California has a benign climate. It is seldom freezing, rarely uncomfortably hot; drizzle is its most depressing natural phenomenon. Richard Fernau and Laura Hartman—here assisted by Jim Axley—had the opportunity to utilize passive solar-heating strategies and conscientiously induced air flow for cooling a new house to be built in this particularly gentle environment. The site was not far from their office in Berkeley, the owner was receptive to innovative approaches to home design, and the young triad of designers began in earnest during the energy-crisis-riddled late 1970s.

The design process began on a two-tier parallel course evidenced in the final built form.

The technical tier was overtly futuristic. Using a British thermodynamics analysis method converted into a computer program called ADMIT, the team began crunching numbers with a vengeance. They were obsessed with analyzing what would happen within the microclimate of the house on any given day.

In a balancing harmony to this heroic assault on scientific truth was the intangible tier of aesthetics. Here both the client and the architects took a long look backward to forms thoroughly alien to the neighboring Grass Valley sophisticates. As the architects reached innocently into the future, experimenting with protoscientific attempts at technical definition, they also delved into a murky past, searching for a house form.

The results are an innocent implementation of technical innovation and a sophisticated deformation of the simple house form generated.

The confluence of these spheres of influence makes for very subtle aesthetic expressions and tangible energy efficiencies. Masonry wall and floor systems are implemented to house a heat-producing Rumford fireplace and provide a thermal flywheel, absorbing the heat provided by the winter sun while absorbing heat provided by the summer air. It would be all too simple to isolate this masonry core, affording it the identity of a segregated appliance, but Fernau and Hartman extended the rationally proportioned and oriented masonry into a variety of elements ranging from the high utility of fireplace to the whimsy of a naked pergola extending out into the light of day. Similarly the historically proportioned and organized house form (patterned loosely upon the alien saltbox) eschews the California Moderne house-as-poignant-jungle-gym but has numerous internal surprises and exterior permutations.

This is a passive solar home designed without a greenhouse, a California house effected without a hot tub, a derivative saltbox that sprouts shed dormers and a sculptural array of venting flues. So many seeming contradictions coalesce in this home simply because neither high tech nor down-home stands pristine and unadulterated by Fernau and Hartman.

However, there is one overriding constant that is in thorough accord with the effort to effect a high degree of energy efficiency and is simultaneously integral to the design of an informal house form. Not surprisingly that common thread is the conscientious planning and design to reduce the volume of the constructed house. Computer printouts and antique engravings substantiate the common cause of creating a small-house form, but it is aesthetic insight that facilitates the lessened sense of constriction that allows a small house to be livable.

ARCHITECTS' STATEMENT

The client, who is fond of vernacular architecture, expressed the desire that the house be sympathetic to its rural surroundings. Although intended for year-round use, the house was to be small and was to utilize passive solar heating and cooling. A masonry fireplace was to be included.

In beginning to design the house, we made a couple of formal decisions: First, that we would start with a simple gable roof form that we would in a sense "remodel" during the design process. This choice was based on the need for economy and an interest in recording the makeshift adaptations that would result from the impact of the thermal criteria on a generic building form. The second decision was that we would divide the house into thermally discrete spaces (rooms). In doing so, we hoped to develop possibilities for control of overheating, underheating, natural convection, and natural ventilation.

Fernau & Hartman

LIST OF PARTICULARS

Brodhead house
Location: La Honda, California
Architects: Fernau & Hartman,
  assisted by Jim Axley
Budget: Not available
Nominal space: 1400 square feet
Perceived space: 1750 square feet

1

Lewis Watts

Figure 1 *Entry, northeast. This is a simple house form: a Cape Cod gable with one corner removed to create entry, the other glazed to present a view. As the house progresses to the west, the saltbox assymmetrically manifests itself. Windows dot the form, sprouting shed dormers. Note the proud multiple-part chimney-flue array at the roof peak. Expressive entry piers begin a march to the world and key entry.*

Figure 2 *North. Entry steps push forth, as the corner hovers above. The window keyed to the entry is merely a screen as it separates the great indoors from the great outdoors. Note how the foundation block work is of the same detailing and material as the exposed chimney above; the exposed vent stack is also an extension of an existing system, the broad-faced clapboard skin.*

Figure 3 *Corner window. Fixed left, venting right, this fenestration motif is repeated throughout the house, facilitating the creative violation of the enclosing box form and limiting its constriction.*

2

3

Lewis Watts

Mark Citret

The Single-Family Residence **59**

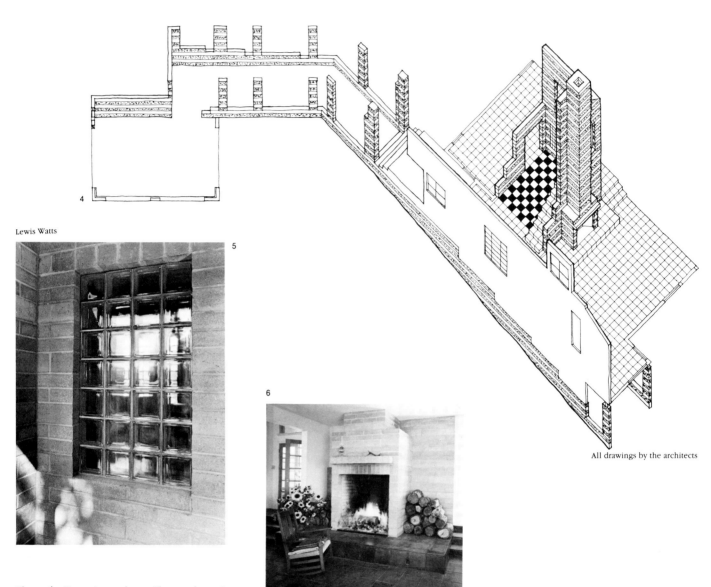

4

Lewis Watts

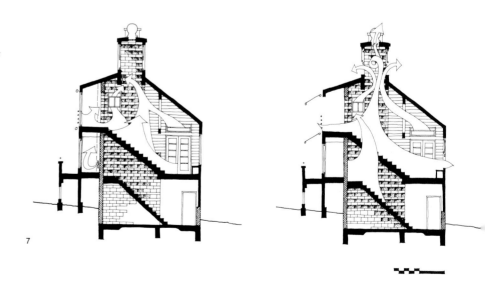

5

6

Mark Citret

All drawings by the architects

Figure 4 *Procession and core. The grand march encounters the solid core as it ascends in positive counterpoint to the linear path. Given the multiple mesh of form, technology, space, and expressive elements, a symbolizing abstraction such as this provides a simple focus for a complex building.*

Figure 5 *Core violation. Glass-block in-fill allows southerly light into the internal core at the point of entry.*

Figure 6 *Fireplace and core. Note the Trombe wall on the right, the Rumford fireplace in the center, and the entry hall on the left. Quarry tile set in concrete absorbs unwanted heat when shaded and absorbs solar heat when the penetrating winter solar angle is allowed to strike its mass. Note the layering of different masonry units to defuse the monolithic potential for mass dominance.*

Figure 7 *Air flow. Winter air flow is shown on the left, summer on the right. Heated air (by fireplace or sun) is stored by the masonry mass and recirculated via the forced-air-duct system. The shaded mass (right) absorbs heat, while hot air is vented by a latter-day cupola. Note the use of transoms to facilitate air flow through discrete spaces.*

7

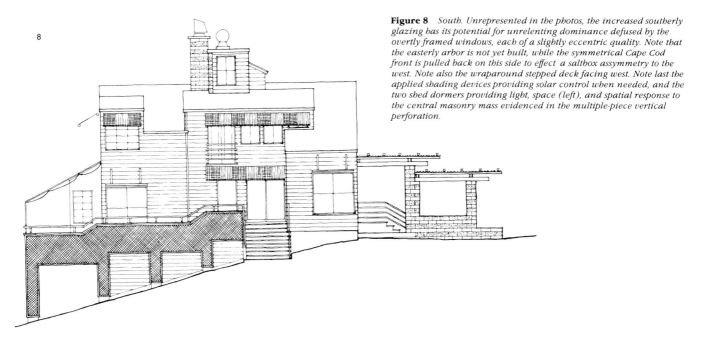

8

Figure 8 *South. Unrepresented in the photos, the increased southerly glazing has its potential for unrelenting dominance defused by the overtly framed windows, each of a slightly eccentric quality. Note that the easterly arbor is not yet built, while the symmetrical Cape Cod front is pulled back on this side to effect a saltbox assymmetry to the west. Note also the wraparound stepped deck facing west. Note last the applied shading devices providing solar control when needed, and the two shed dormers providing light, space (left), and spatial response to the central masonry mass evidenced in the multiple-piece vertical perforation.*

Axes, the vertical release of space, applied extensions of the built form, and expressive detailing are subtly interwoven by the designers to effect a home at ease with its 1400 square feet. The essential description of the parts employed reveals a consistent rejection of a dominant element or space in favor of a sophisticated mesh.

An extended entry promenade starts at an outbuilding and translates into a pergola of freestanding masonry piers leading to a front door covered with a double-cantilevered corner. Beyond the threshold and the slight squeeze encountered at entry, the ceiling is allowed to ascend to the roof underside along this extended processional bay. The increased space allows for the perception of the second grand-scale element employed by Fernau and Hartman, the aggrandized masonry mass, centered à la saltbox planning but extruded à la Trombe wall engineering.

The promenade-cum-datum thus embraces the central masonry hub, which in turn subdivides the remaining first-floor spaces of kitchen–dining room and living room. Applied to the simple rectangular plan profile are a deck and two bay extensions (one accommodating dining, the other extending the promenade bay).

The central stair further melds the masonry core and the vertical entry space as it leads up through the extruded concrete block wall. As it does on the first floor, the central core divides two spaces on the second, appropriately isolating sleeping spaces. The single bath is harbored within the crux of stair and chimney but held distinct from both the stair and the entry space it sits above by several feet of unencumbered space.

Around and through all these elements are linking axes and carefully placed windows providing spatial relief and an ordering influence. All these gentle aesthetic pyrotechnics have formal consequences. Shed dormers harbor windows and create intimate spaces within the context of a steeply pitched roof springing from a low eave height. Corner windows provide visual release as well.

The creation of either a technological marvel or the architectural photocopy of an antique farmhouse would have involved far less sensitivity, sophistication, and angst. By melding the twin worlds of science and history into a condensed house form conveying extraordinary aesthetic insight, Fernau and Hartman have embraced a maximum number of influences while maintaining architectural credibility.

By rejecting the myopic focus of exclusive preoccupation in favor of an ambiguously lyric composition of disparate influences, Richard Fernau and Laura Hartman have evidenced the very best quality architects have to offer: perspective. Raw creativity can prove errantly zealous. Technical expertise can diffuse aesthetic potential. But perspective provides the means for human beings to gain control over their actions.

Gentle Eccentricity

*Young New York designers create a tiny house of perfect fit,
subtle detailing, and genuine poignance in rural Maine.*

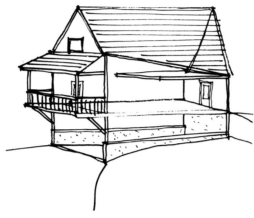

Innocence is an elusive commodity. Folk art is simple and yet richly rewarding. In architecture, undesigned, indigenous buildings can gain considerable charm from their ad hoc construction. However, feigned innocence in architecture, art, and human affairs is poisonous to trust and grating to the senses.

How do college-educated, striving professionals encounter the raw grace of rural Maine with a sympathetic aesthetic vision? Much depends upon the fit between designers and client and between the designers' egos and the nature of the design criteria.

From the images presented in this book, it is obvious that this house has a presence both unique and familiar, not unlike that of the very best folk art. There are subtleties and sophistications in this house rarely found in uninformed construction. As with all extraordinary art, the multiple meanings and enriching counterpoints of the Hog Hill house offer a depth of vision and expression both powerful and lyrically intriguing.

The designers of this house are architectural youngsters Ronald D. Bentley, Salvatore LaRosa, and Franklin Salasky. An empathy with their young clients—a couple with a new baby—can be assumed.

The intimacy of the design process began with a 2-year ownership and development of the site prior to building. Essentially the future home owners were civilizing the wilderness, and they became very familiar with the area, experiencing the entire range of natural extremes inland Maine has to offer.

It is with the simplest of programs (a small house for a young family) and the most meager of budgets (well under $50,000) that the design process had its start. Infused with the spirit of ingenuous informality that is the hallmark of rural domestic design, the collaboration of 3 designers, 2½ clients, and 1 very poetic site brought forth a singularly unforgettable building.

A dry description of the elements that resulted from such a fertile field of creative input may not convey fully the unspoken warmth and poignance obvious in the images depicted but is nonetheless dutifully attempted.

Essentially a three-part vertical layering, the house has a symmetrical beginning and end. Viewed from afar, the prosaic gable-end exterior has the proud rustication of a hardworking down-easter. Viewed architecturally, the thoroughly dynamic triad of different windows somehow rotating about the simple, stock front door which is centered on the gable and harbored beneath a shed roof, creates a lyric dialogue between that which is actively irrational and that which is in considered repose.

The internal response to this exterior interplay is similarly intriguing. The house is entered above the basement plinth and below the floating loft. An axial orientation, which responds to the latently centered entry facade is encountered immediately. The entry to the house is released via orientation to an opposing door, but it is also horizontally pinched by the presence of 6 × 12 inch loft-floor framing above. The informality of the entry facade is echoed in the internal detailing of the exposed framing and floor underside.

Essentially, the entry floor houses all public functions of cooking, eating, and socializing. The freestanding loft accommodates the isolated functions of children's play and musical rehearsal.

DESIGNERS' STATEMENT

Our clients, a couple in their late twenties with a young son, decided to build a house they could afford now yet live in for the rest of their lives. A great deal of time was spent deciding how this house should be designed from both a functional and an aesthetic point of view, knowing that the house was to be the nucleus of a homestead to be developed over time.

The modest budget dictated a house of very little square footage, so we reached a decision to make the major living spaces as open as possible, compromising on the size and number of bedrooms as well as storage areas. Future outbuildings were anticipated: a woodshed, a small barn, and a garage would eventually be built.

Ronald D. Bentley

LIST OF PARTICULARS

Hog Hill house
Location: Rural Maine
Designers: Bentley/LaRosa/Salasky
Budget: $48,000
Nominal space: 1400 square feet
Perceived space: 1700 square feet

1

All photos and drawings courtesy of the architects

2

Figure 1 *South. As the hill trails off to the left, the roof eave correspondingly ascends, accommodating the shed-covered deck. A simple dialogue is effected between strip glazing above and point glazing for the lower floor. Two facade elements create a sense of designed integration on this elevation: first, the alignment of the eave of the deck roof and the top edge of the strip window glazing; second, the use of an abstracted, outsize window to terminate the strip. Multiple foci of deck, pediment above deck, and 6 × 6 foot window allow the transitional roof to be an embracing idiosyncrasy rather than a naked gesture.*

Figure 2 *East, entry. Front door, symmetrical roof peak, and shed overhang center a face that has considered enlivening absurdity added in the form of three antigravitational, unrelated, standard windows dancing about the gable-defined center.*

3

Figure 3 *Loft views. Attached over the entry, this simple platform (top) is made unforgettable by the transitional ceiling plane, pinched at entry, lofting toward the balcony edge (left). All elements of rail, window, chimney, and stair are given room to breathe; because the floor plane is held distinct from the side walls, a dissociative spatial float is achieved. Note the lightly vertical eccentric window on the entry gable in counterpoint to the lightly horizontal window proudly centered on the deck gable. Note also the suspended tie-rod beyond the balcony rail. Note last the indigenous raw pine trim, flooring, and rail.*

Figure 4 *West. A proud deck affords a tree-house view. Note that 4 × 10 inch knee bracing replaces columnar support.*

4

5

6

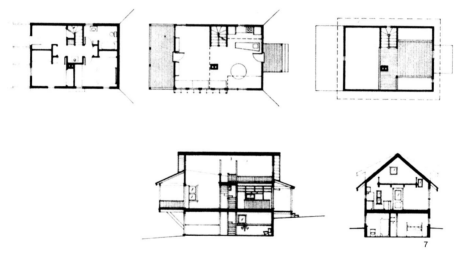

7

Figure 5 *Northeast. Scattered windows, no two alike, perforate a tight little house form. Note the stringlike datum interacting, avoiding, and finally defining window locations. This datum is simply a painted drip cap between identically stained cedar shingles above and tongue-and-groove siding below.*

Figure 6 *Interior, south wall. A grand-scale element is created simply by aligning the window tops. The wall and ceiling are liberated by using timbers to support the loft (upper left). Note the considered application of a window (center) located to both vent hot summer air and highlight the beam face. Note also the minor tie-rod connection into the beam face described. The lowering of the windowsill height at the dining area creates a subspace simply because the natural illumination is differentiated. The loft-deck edge and rail are unapologetically rustic and plain, with each part given room to express itself.*

Figure 7 *Plans and sections. Plans (above) begin at bottom floor (left) and ascend to the roof (right), while the longitudinal section (bottom left) and transverse section (bottom right) allow the innards to be inspected. The partially buried plinth-basement houses two bedrooms, nestled to catch southerly solar gain and view while warming their back walls to a central wood stove. Utility room, stair, and bath fill out the plan. The open entry floor has only the stair and kitchen as plan intrusions, while the loft (dashed lines) provides horizontal containment over the entry. The loft allows the walls and the ceiling to remain relatively untouched. The sections best describe the floating loft, while showing the constant ridge line and constantly ascending wall plate line. Note the knee-braced support for the deck; the open, heavy-timber framing for the loft floor; and the roof-pitch transition indicated by the dashed lines on the transverse section.*

The most obvious element of reinvention occurs in the roof form, a form that is directly translated to the unencumbered ceiling above both loft and living area. The task in low-budget house design is not merely the reduction of building size but also the creative reapplication of standard framing technologies that effect innovation at a minimum cost. The roof of the Hog Hill house is the single most memorable reinvention in this book.

A centered entry is best effected set in a steeply pitched gable end of a house. An expansive external view is best perceived when the integral space addresses the view horizontally. At one end, the Hog Hill house presents the centered entry described; at the other end, a cathedralized living room and covered porch focus our eyes horizontally to the treetops captured above the falling ground plane beyond the house. A vertically expressive gable at one end translates into a horizontally expansive gable at the other. A simple transition is effected by keeping the roof ridge line constant while raising the exterior wall plate line. The roof and ceiling planes warp as each rafter pitch varies to maintain ridge height and eave overhang. Front and back are thus a literal and linear transition, inside and out.

The results as seen from the loft prospect are both disconcerting and thoroughly enchanting. Soft spatial swelling is held in unapologetic contrast to the rather prosaic loft rail and decking, and kept totally distinct via the heavy framing support below. All surfaces are intimately touchable and thoroughly familiar. And yet the effect is slightly fantastic or dreamlike because of the internal billowing of the ceiling plane.

The north side has several diminutive and scattered windows, the dominant element being a corner window inextricably combined with the deck and accommodating a sweeping view. The west end has a single dominant element in the form of a covered deck. The elevated eave described facilitates an integral shed roof overhang beneath the raised-gable roof form. This overhang completely covers the view-oriented deck, a deck that extends the fair-weather utility of the living area. It is the south side where the glazing organization becomes an overtly designed element. In Maine, anything that fosters heat is a friendly aspect. The southern facade of ganged, double-hung windows terminating in an abstracted square of 6 × 6 foot fixed glazing both embraces the sun and provides a sense of conspired integrity to the house's intentions and realization. The only custom glazing present in the house, this window compositionally mirrors the covered end of the deck to the west.

If there is a "black box" amid all the overt expressiveness, it is the hidden plinth of two bedrooms and a bath that supports the poetry described. Unrepresented in the photographs available, the semi-earth-covered floor "takes care of business," housing the utility room, wood stove, solitary bath, and two tiny bedrooms.

A deeper level of detailing further enhances the intentions of the house. Facades of seemingly chaotic window placement can distract a cursory encounter to the point where examined inconsistency can be mistaken for careless nonchalance. Bentley, LaRosa, and Salasky avoid such misconceptions by the careful combination of exterior material types and textures, blended by a dark stain. The use of a wrap-around datum in the form of a painted drip cap at the interface between shingled upper face and vertical tongue-and-groove lower face helps define the scale of the windows and provides a designed contextual reference for the busy informality. An abstracted steel-rod lattice over the southerly glazing adds an element of detached detail to the homogeneous integration of the elements described.

The Hog Hill house is quite simply a brilliant example of timeless integrity and personal vision. The kinetics of roof form, window orientation, and second-floor organization are thoroughly embraced by the familiarity of materials, techniques, and detailing.

A singular vision can become a grotesque abstraction, while a distracted embrace of unrelated elements can become a muddy mess of mediocrity. Casting a blind eye to the existing world betrays an arrogant ignorance. Being cowed by history and context preempts creativity and produces insensitive replication.

Architecture at its best can have a firm foundation of essential truth as well as the liberation of expressed innovation. The familiar can dance with the unprecedented, and the Hog Hill house is indeed choreographed to display the results of that interplay. By aligning and juxtaposing standard elements in fresh ways, limiting reinventions to the roof and outsize dining area window, and carefully detailing standard exterior surface treatments, this young triad of designers focuses upon those qualities of small-house architecture that capture our hearts and minds.

In denying the validity of extremism in favor of the contrapuntal harmonies of an invigorated small house, Bentley, LaRosa, and Salasky have presented a unique vision. Enhanced by its minimum of means, this house needs no apologetic explanations. Instead the Hog Hill house evidences a pride and life made possible by sensitive articulation of genuine creativity.

Rising Pride

A young builder hires a young architect to help him express his skill and house a growing family.

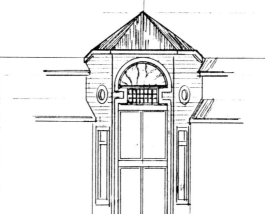

Ralph Indorf is a builder in Westchester County, New York. He is also a father of a young son and a husband to Cathy May Indorf. Several years ago, with a growing family and business, his thoughts turned to accommodation, or the lack thereof, of his home and business.

Being familiar with construction, Ralph realized that there is no mystique to designing a house. He contacted a designer referred to him by one of his material suppliers. Ralph had much to convey to this young practitioner and left their first meeting with high hopes of realizing his dream house the next time they met. They did indeed meet again, but the house was not Ralph's dream. In fact the house was anything but a dreamy creation; rather, the home divined by this designer was so rooted in gratuitous mundanity that it left Ralph cold.

Discouraged but undaunted, Ralph hit upon the notion of asking a young architect to give him a hand. They had recently worked together on a small project and seemed to have formed a relationship of mutual respect. To Ralph's surprise the architect was eager to help and willing to let his fee be minimized. If bid drawings need not be prepared, if construction documents are needed only to obtain a building permit rather than keep a builder honest, and if an architect does not have to perform site inspections, then the time needed for the project greatly diminishes (as should the architect's fee). It should be noted that *someone* must perform site inspections and prepare careful working drawings. Without these things being taken care of, no rational architect would be the architect of record on any project, given the potential for unknowing liability.

LIST OF PARTICULARS

Indorf house
Location: Yorktown Heights, New York
Architect: Duo Dickinson
Budget: $125,000 (estimated retail)
Nominal space: 1500 square feet
Perceived space: 2100 square feet

The architect took Ralph's sketches, visited the site, scribbled a bit, and in short order gave him a preliminary scheme. Although the scheme contained most if not all of Ralph's and Cathy May's thoughts, the architect's sketches reflected an entirely new thrust and image neither Ralph nor his first designer had been able to envision.

Perhaps it is best to articulate the difference between the words "designer" and "architect." Any aware human being capable of semirational thought may be called a "designer." An architect, not unlike a doctor or lawyer, is tested and licensed by a state board. An architect must either apprentice for 9 years with a licensed practitioner or get a professional degree (a 3-year masters's or a 5-year bachelor's) and then apprentice for 3 years before he or she is allowed to take the licensing tests—tests that actually do limit the number of those getting licenses.

There are indeed many architects who are simply inept in one professional area or another. But there are almost no designers who can begin to bring more than rudimentary drafting skills to any phase of the design process. You get what you pay for, and designers are indeed cheaper than architects.

With all this said, it may be best to address the building effected by the builder-architect collaboration.

First and foremost, the home was to be designed to take advantage of a passive solar potential by orienting 90 percent of its glazing to the south. Second, the home had to accommodate an office for Ralph Indorf's contracting company. Third, the home was to be built with only one bedroom and bath but in such a way that it could be expanded or developed into a house that would ultimately con-

Figure 1 *South. Windows are arrayed to form strip glazing, composed to form focal points, and positioned in blissful ignorance as needed. The tower (left) receives the animated living wing (right) and awaits the ultimate construction of a second wing (left).*

2

3

Figure 2 *Entry, north. Somewhat cryptic, energy-efficient in its paucity of windows, and ultimately alluring for its quietly expressive presence, this sweet form is a quiet combination of form and geometry. Note the simplest indication of the tower (center top).*

Figure 3 *Entry, west. Lopsided in its anticipation of an addition (to the right), this shape is both enigmatic and homespun.*

Figure 4 *East. Stock windows conspire to be ornament in a tall facade. Note the heavy overhang (right) and the simple extension of the corner to form a chimney.*

4

tain 3 bedrooms and 2½ baths. All of these features were brought into the project's design criteria by Ralph and Cathy May Indorf. Not surprisingly the architect's responses evidenced much of what this book is trying to convey.

The architect formed the long axis of the home along the east-west ordinate, creating the now-unsurprising broad south face. Given the north-south axis of site entry, a north-facing front door would have been the most expedient entry. But expediency is the mother of mediocrity, and the architect opted to enter from the west end, allowing for an uninterrupted 50-foot axis visible as one crosses the threshold.

Similarly, the first image of a house presented to a visitor is normally a centering embrace of grand welcome. But given the northerly approach, glazing facing the site access was greatly limited. Rather than try to falsify a gesture of welcome, the architect enhanced the mystery implicit in inaccessibility by creating a thoroughly extraordinary roof form. Essentially, the open (and private) southern facade needed a raised eave height to accept adequate glazing for proper solar penetration. The north side had the opposite imperative: not only was glazing undesirable, prominent protrusions simply radiate heat, so the young architect brought the northerly eave height down to the lowest point that would maintain full utility of the second floor. By extending the eave to a dramatic 4-foot knee-braced overhang, the architect further lowered the eave and enhanced the enigmatic opacity encountered upon entry.

The blank north facade, indirect west entry, and expressive roof form all create a great deal of anticipation prior to actual entry, and there had to be some form of payoff for all the built-up expectation. As mentioned, the entry axis presents a grand vista, but a horizontal axis is indeed a transitional phenomenon—beckoning, releasing, but not rewarding. For this expert gesture of spiritual reward, the architect saved the single unforgettable aspect of his design.

At the transition from north side to west side of the house, the roof forms a simple hip resolution of the double-pitched corner. This diagonal line was extended by the architect beyond the roof peak to form a corner tower of proud projection above the norm for domestic architecture. The projecting form as seen from the north only heightens the sense of veiled spatial promises as expressed in exterior form.

On the interior this tower form encloses a vertical shaft of space and light of unprecedented impact for a home of 1500 square feet. The tower space is incidental to the entry axis (not its focus) and thus is made more surprising

5

6

7

Figure 5 *Balcony. Leading to the master bedroom, this spatial and formal link gives scale to the ascendant tower space. Note the variety of visible spaces and windows.*

Figure 6 *Entry axis. This is the major horizontal link throughout the entire length of the house. Note the glow of the tower (right) and the distant bay window (center) beckoning the entrant. Note also the heavy-timber balcony framing above the axis.*

Figure 7 *Tower. The central focus of the entire house interior, this massive space convects solar-heated air to bedrooms above.*

as it is revealed only upon complete processional immersion into the house's interior. The tower space forms a couplet with the lower-level horizontal living room, which *is* the focal point of the entry axis. The horizontal-vertical spatial dance creates a dynamic flow of space throughout the entire volume of the house. The tower functionally accommodates the dining area, but in truth its main identity is that of spiritual heart and soul for the home, as all spaces feed from its dominant presence.

Ancillary spaces of kitchen, storage, and stair provide separating spatial in-fill between the tower and the other walls. A cross axis from the stair between the dining and kitchen spaces to the backyard beyond enriches a potentially relentless focus.

The second floor harbors an east-facing master bedroom suite above the living area and stakes out space for a children's bedroom and bath above the kitchen. The stair is directly oriented to the central tower space, enhancing its impact. Wrapping about the two homeward sides of the tower space is a balcony accessing all the second-story spaces. A custom rail of expressive pieces and parts provides physical restraint and visual richness.

Other specialized aspects employed by the architect are in the form of window orientations. Southerly windows form strip glazing along the east wing (living room and bedroom), while the tower reinforces its angular symmetry and height with a multiple-window array culminating in a large half-round far window. The east wall of the master bedroom has a similarly expressive array utilizing stock window elements in a fresh and invigorating way.

The entire east-end basement under the living room is given over to the mandatory office. Room for expansion is provided by the blank south wall opposite the kitchen. Once the planned-for wing has been effected—creating an additional bedroom above and a den below—the tower's posture will become even more crucial to the entire composition. Whereas the present building uses the tower ascension to define one corner, the additional wing will provide the formal pinch from which the tower will ascend.

Figure 8 *Master bedroom. The final reward for the grand march of circulation, this simple array is both active and centered.*

8

The multiple identities of this project all emerge from under one roofscape and a simple rectangular perimeter with one modest fold in its outline. Variety and power are evoked from the prioritization of the elements demanded in the program provided by the Indorfs. A tower is created simply by extending a roofline and condensing second-floor space to create a void below the ascending form. Similarly, an axis that reveals and orders the entire house is created by orienting the entry to bypass the stair and locating its center to a distant bay window.

These steps are not inherently costly. Indeed in one sense the added amenity has a thoroughly intangible value, depending on the subjective worth of spirituality in the spaces created.

It is only with the implementation of perspective and professional skill that such results can be effected. Good intentions and drafting skills cannot compensate for the lack of ability to perceive form and space abstractly. The ability to manipulate building parts to empower a small house beyond its defined size is not genetically derived or accidentally imparted. Training, experience, and a commitment to the concept of maximum benefits from minimum resources are essential.

There are always people willing to give of their time to help effect the design of a house—a relative, a contractor, a decorator, or some other helpful person on the fringe of design expertise—but the level of perspective provided by training and experience offered by an architect is indispensable to the creation of a maximally impactive and utilitarian small house.

As the house grows to accommodate a growing family and business, the Indorfs will implement that far-reaching professional insight. Without their modest investment to purchase perspective, the prospect would be somewhat distressing. Instead, theirs is a positive realization that their home is under control and in the process of reaching its potential.

9

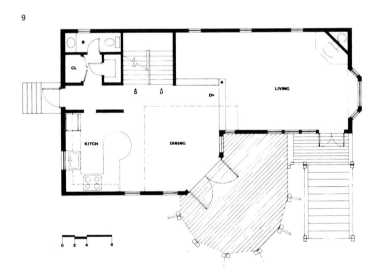

Figure 9 *Plans. The longitudinal entry axis is counterpointed by the vertical axis of the dining room tower space. Note that a two-bedroom addition is contemplated for the southwest corner of the house (lower left); this would create a central posture for the tower.*

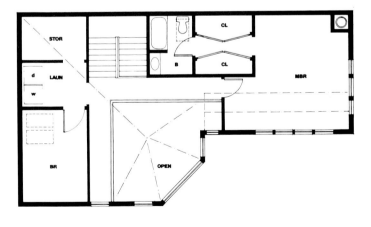

Drawings by Clay Eicher

Towering Influence

Daniel J. Cinelli builds a tower and surrounds it with space to form a house.

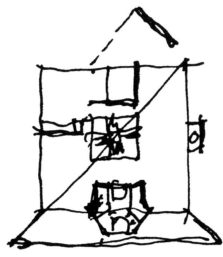

I n the design of a small house, there is often truth in illusion. The creation of axial links that perceptually combine spaces within the limits of a strict spatial diet affords psychic release without the cost of added volume. Similarly, the creative juxtaposition or isolation of common elements of a home provides a sense of refreshing delight, thus mitigating the potential for constriction without adding costly custom fabrication.

The home Daniel J. Cinelli designed for Tom and Chris Meyer and their child on a site in Lake Bluff, Illinois, has these elements and also has the added benefits of solar orientation and a literal extension of the vertical dimension, all creating an efficient, ingenious house of thoughtful interactivity.

Essentially, a square plan with a central square tower enclosing the stair defines a simple house form. The extraordinary developments occur when the latent potentials of the concentric squares are made manifest by the architect. A square's diagonals form a 45° cross axis. Cinelli extends this diagonal to form the triangulated second-floor plan. The central stair is by nature a vertical form, hence, the objectification of this plan element into a literal tower form—complete with interior facades—is a reasonable fantasy realized. When the expressed tower and divined diagonal organizing lines for the house form meet at the roof, lyric ambiguity is achieved.

The centered tower form ascends through one double-hipped roof only to encounter another. The effect is of a dynamic roof stretching to contain the tower's ascendance, with the single-story portion as a sheared leftover.

A third extension of roof and imagination occurs at the overt front of the

ARCHITECT'S STATEMENT

Tom and Chris Meyer, who constructed most of the house themselves, wanted something at the outset that most of us desire: 3000 square feet of space for the price of 1500 square feet.

The Meyer house seems wider and larger than it really is because the front symmetrical solar screen wall and the dual porticos have been elongated and projected against the angular backdrop of the second floor. To give a feeling of additional volume, I designed the stair tower as a house within a house, thus allowing endless views of other rooms through the eyeglass windows. Rooms also gain functional elements; the traditional living room, for example, contains separate conversation and music areas and a reading alcove.

The Meyer residence is my response to what I believe homes should be called upon to provide: Housing with quality spaces and illusions toward a larger scale. Both inside and out, housing should be affordable, energy-efficient, and most of all exciting to be in.

Daniel J. Cinelli

LIST OF PARTICULARS

Meyer house
Location: Lake Bluff, Illinois
Architect: Daniel J. Cinelli
Budget: $70,000 (owner-built)
Nominal space: 2000 square feet
Perceived space: 2560 square feet

house, facing south. Small houses benefit from extensions of form that create illusions of scale; these applied parts are both aggrandizing and functionally utilitarian.

In this case, the south-facing front of the house has an extended false-front portico, serving to create protected space and provide solar shading. Aesthetically the peekaboo quality of a void-violated, freestanding wall creates a sense of depth missing in a simple prismatic massing. Cinelli accepts the opportunity presented by the portico to extend the hexagonal entry air lock into the covered space.

Thus tower, sheared roof, extended portico, and air lock combine to effect a considered formal collision of expressed parts. If left at this point, the design would be hypothetically intriguing but essentially devoid of domestic sensibility or human scale.

Cinelli next applies a layer of spatial linkage and expressive detailing that enriches this polygonal interplay beyond the point of detached kinetics. At the entry, interior window openings in the form of a consistently centered array are aligned to form an uninterrupted visual axis through the entire house height up into the clerestory-lit tower top. Beyond the initial encounter, entry further reveals the proudly presented central tower form, containing openings on all exposed sides similar to those already revealed at the threshold. These windows are in truth openings with applied muntins, devoid of glass. They are slightly reduced from normal window size to enhance the vertical pull of the internal tower element. Cinelli has made the tower more than simply the enclosure for a stair; he has given it the luxury of a little added spatial volume, enough

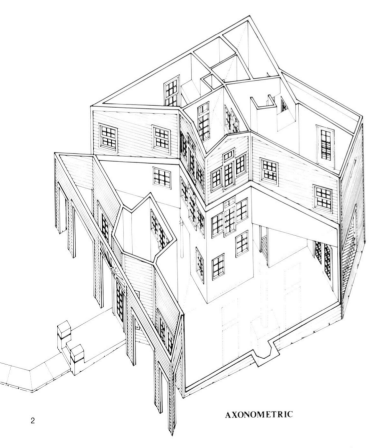

AXONOMETRIC

Figure 1   *South, entry. Portico and tower top dominate the skewed house form, key entry, and internal focus of the house.*

Figure 2   *Axonometric. Extended entry portico, incised and bias-sheared form, and ascendant tower are natural products of the square-plan motif employed. Note how both bedrooms gain clerestory lighting from the tower top.*

Figure 3   *Entry. A positive address of the imminent human encounter, the bulging centered form is barely contained behind the applied freestanding screen-wall. Note the beckoning tower top beyond, gathering in the diagonal second-story wall and centering the entire house form.*

4

5

Figure 4 *The positive focus. The realized tower is scaled as an independent exterior form but detailed as an interior lantern and spatial focus. The size of the upper windows has been reduced below expectations to enhance the sense of height. The roof-underside ceiling is effectively stretched taut by the tower ascension. Note the sea of tile floor and flood of space that allow for the objectification of the tower element as a freestanding architectural element.*

Figure 5 *Entry pinch. Air lock (left) and tower (right) address each other, and clerestory windows diagonally opposing each other allow for the perceived entry axis. This simple reduction in width divides dining room (beyond) from living room (foreground).*

Figure 6 *Axis. The orientation of the living room to the back door and deck beyond this linear release defies the spatial limitations of the house. Punctured by openings, the tower form reveals top-lit space beckoning beyond. Note the diagonal imposition of the second floor (above, right), aiding the axial impact and definition.*

Figure 7 *Axis (again). This view back through the living room shows how the axis works in two directions. Note the nonglazed, muntin-divided opening and stair tower to the right, keying its quiet power.*

6

7

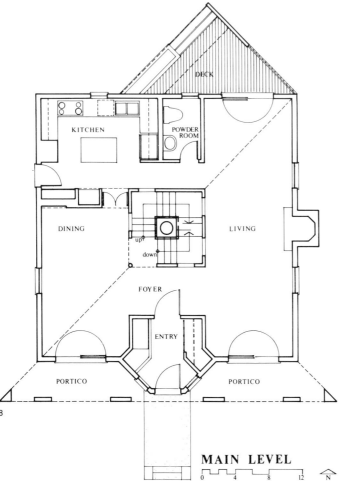

Figure 8 *Plans. The main level (left) reveals a square within a square, as the central tower orients entry, subdivides the first floor, and provides access to the other four levels. Note the freestanding extended portico and positive entry air lock. The elongated living area stretches spatial scale and is easily subdividable. The upper level (below) becomes triangular as the square plan's diagonal is formally manifest. Note that the smallish bedrooms have their constriction relieved by vaulted ceilings. Note the back-to-back baths oriented above the first-floor wet areas. Note how the extended master bedroom corner defeats the constriction of the oblique corners defined by the diagonal as the deck further extends the perceived space. Note how the tower has interior-facing openings overlooking the open space above the living and dining areas.*

Figure 9 *The spatial hub. Given an open ambience, the tower interior is not simply a space to accommodate stairs. Exterior light cascades down through the shaft of air. Note the square air-recirculating duct used to retrieve solar-heated air in winter. Operable windows above serve to vent hot summer air, effectively draining the house of unwanted heat.*

Figure 10 *Section. The aligned clerestory windows connect the entry, foyer, tower, and bedroom spaces, creating a space-relieving axis. Note also the column of space contained by the tower, which serves to distribute diffused light internally, vent hot air in summer, and recirculate heated air in winter. Note also how the bedroom has its roof angled to address the tower space. Note last how the extension decks of the back and the bedroom relieve the squeeze.*

MAIN LEVEL

0   4   8   12   N

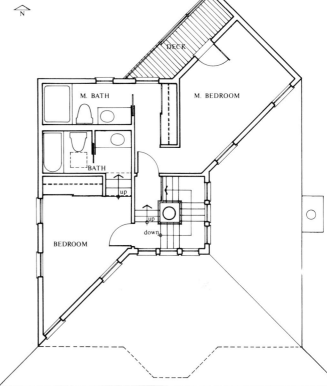

UPPER LEVEL

0   4   8   12   N

for it to read as a shaft of space rather than a simple functional accommodation. Clerestory light from the tower top filters down through the defined shaft. As light descends, space ascends, and above the wraparound living areas the ceiling is fairly pulled taut by the vertical force of the aspiring form.

Being a conscientious designer, Cinelli exploited the potential of his interior formal folly with some utilitarian air-moving features. Hot air is vented in summer and collected and recycled in winter by the columnar mass of air. The tower also creates a vertical spatial axis, relieving the sense of limited space.

Just as the tower orients the dynamics of the exterior form, so it orders interior space. It pinches the defined space between its form and the entry air lock to divide the dining room from the living room. The last leftover corner of the square plan is given over to the wet functions of kitchen and bath.

Two cross axes link living and dining rooms, and kitchen and dining room, helping to extend perceived space. A modest deck is applied to the north side as well. The second floor manifests the implicit diagonal cross axis of the square plan as its major formal delineator, allowing the orthogonal tower to express its form to the outside world. Two bedrooms are inserted into the remote corners of the triangular plan effected, with the master bedroom gaining space from a squaring of the oblique corner to create a fully-formed master bedroom and a small balcony. The remaining squared corner above the first-floor kitchen and bath is given over to two baths.

The basement takes up two-thirds of the house plan on its level; the remaining third, to the south, is simply a slab on grade foundation and is defined by the tower south wall. It is used for a heat sink, holding solar gain for winter and cooling summer heat by its shaded mass, a classic thermal flywheel.

It is with the utilitarian application of energy-efficient technology and the considered elaboration on the square-plan motif that this scheme transcends the awkward potential of literal geometry imposed on a house form.

It is the tower that controls all formal focus and spatial orientation. It is the tower, set in a small sea of space, that extends the impact of this small house beyond the level of expectation.

Indicated upon entry, revealed upon occupancy, the full impact of the crucial tower imposition can only be appreciated by the ongoing interface between humanity and architecture as the house is used. An unforgettable image, the tower is indeed the heart of the entire composition.

It is in the creation of a home with a heart that an architect utilizes the best of what he or she has to offer. In this case Daniel J. Cinelli has created literal fantasy in a tangible form. The family housed had a focus for the months of construction and more importantly for the ongoing years of turning a small building into a home.

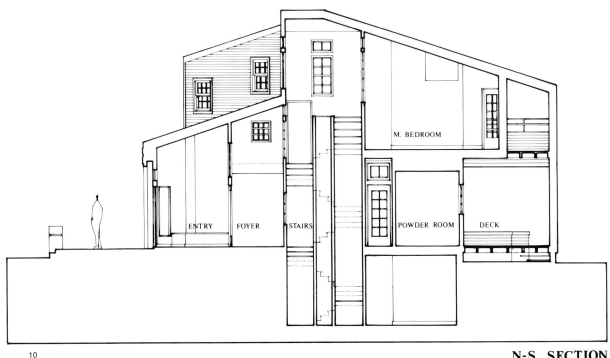

10

N-S SECTION

Pieces and Parts

William Lipsey makes a modest home memorable with some considered discontinuities.

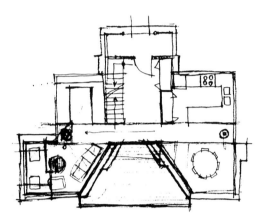

Dodge City has become apochryphal in its imagery. False fronts, stage-set Victorian detailing, and blankly subdominant massing—perhaps a bit hazy in a black-and-white, cathode-ray-tube-filtered memory—are conjured up by the very mention of this wild-west context. Aspen, Colorado, though far away in time and space from Dodge City, is a living reminder that such honky-tonk, kinetically crude and yet innocently brazen architecture has an undeniable appeal.

William Lipsey is an architect who enjoys creating the sense of mannered distortion quite reminiscent of our rough-and-ready past. Formal animation, aggressive and passive pieces and parts, and multiple finish treatments create a lively living environment in his work.

It is that liveliness, that energetic spirit of potential volatility that helps this 2100-square-foot house accommodate four bedrooms without the depressing sense of spatial limitation.

Lipsey has taken an extruded-gable form and has violated its mass while applying extraneous elements with an innocence that is exuberant. The formal negations have been made manifest by truncating the roof peak (creating an octagonal geometry echoed throughout the building) and by excising the central third of the view-oriented half of the house (creating an outdoor "room" thoroughly embraced by the building).

These two negations are complemented by two equally assertive addenda. The living room launches an applied bay (overtly peculiar only in its place in the home), and the entry, also an appliqué, again suspended above the ground and proudly formed in contradistinction to the main domestic mass.

ARCHITECT'S STATEMENT

Three main concerns centered my thoughts about this project:

1. I wanted to do a contemporary house that would be well-liked by virtue of incorporating, in a subtle and indirect way, proven patterns of the past. The old Victorian miners' houses in Aspen enjoy a universal appeal. I suspect the attraction has to do with the eye-catching liveliness of the surfaces and the masses.

2. I wanted to do a house that had interesting proportions—a house whose spaces and shapes had the "right stuff" inside and out, from every angle.

3. I wanted to pursue my interest in ambiguous imagery. The flat, entry side of the house has overtones of a frontier false-front while from other angles the house suggests boatlike images.

William Lipsey

LIST OF PARTICULARS

Ma house
Location: Aspen, Colorado
Architect: William Lipsey
Budget: $135,000
Nominal space: 2100 square feet
Perceived space: 2600 square feet

There is indeed method to the seemingly immodest posturing of this house. Access to this hillside home is accommodated best at a second-story level. Given the potential for solar gain present in a south-facing hillside in Colorado, a shallow building section was called for, and hence a tall house form resulted in order to accommodate the essential square footage. With four bedrooms to be dealt with, including a master bedroom suite, the entry level was given over completely to the public spaces of kitchen, dining room, and living room, having its spread sandwiched between two floors of sleeping accommodations.

A Colorado home without a sun-drenched deck is like a ski slope in August—limited in utility. Because of the second-story posture of the living space, an attached deck would have been far above the descending slope of the hill, so Lipsey eliminated enclosed deck space in favor of a lofted courtyard incised between living and eating spaces and centered upon entry. The internal spatial requirements imposed by the tight plan perimeter forced the additive application of the living and entry bays described. The push-me-pull-you aspects of this planning are in thorough harmony with the fresh exuberance of the innocently brash aesthetics of a bygone era Lipsey is so enamored with.

Given the unapologetic directness of his formal manipulations, Lipsey then set out to create an overtly modern home. Windows were broad-planed and full-width to exploit views and the heating solar penetration. Exposed laminated wood beams collected second-story loads, facilitating a thoroughly open public floor plan. The entire third floor is given over to a multiple-space master

Figure 1 *West. The sunset-capturing living room extension seemingly sticks its face out into the light. Note the wagon-wheel–ship's-wheel windows set into the massive clapboard facade on the north side of the house.*

Figure 2 *Entry, northeast. A decorated box has windows flecked upon its form. The entry is recognized by the bared tin flashing and drip edge which forms architectural bas-relief. Note the entry bridge. Formally this appears to be a truncated gable roof; in truth the entry bay (right) is a simple addition to a house mass capped by a shed roof (left) and a flat peak (center).*

Figure 3 *Southwest. As the hill trails off to the right, a proud assemblage of parts seems to reach out to embrace the unlimited view. Note the unapologetic wing, overtly tacked on to the house form and supported by a cross-braced column couplet. Note also the repeated octagonal window-top motif repeated throughout the home.*

All photos by Gordon H. Schenck, Jr.

4

Figure 4 *Living area. A window wall wraps about the entire south side, as a large social deck is incised into the form, and a balcony extends from the master bedroom. Space is allowed to rise up under the roof underside. Note the exterior-style interior openings to the lofted master bedroom. The ceiling is wood, while a carefully placed skylight relieves the oblique focus of the ceiling plane and provides light to a potential black hole.*

Figure 5 *Stair. Pieces and parts are gingerly applied to the monolithic gypsum-board walls. Note the spatial projection of the applied westerly bay in left background, and the custom-crafted wood stove mimicking the geometrics of the octagonal openings. Note also the heavy timber beam across the void created by the applied bay.*

Figure 6 *Plans. In the basement (top), three bedrooms are clustered around the stair access and bath. The entry (middle) has flanking living (left) and kitchen-eating (right) spaces. Intruding into the plan, providing spatial release upon entry, is the imposing social deck. Note the extensive southern glazing and the repeating eccentricities of implied symmetry continually violated as the house parts interact, producing the living room bay extension to the west (left), the locally centered front door (top), and the lightly eccentric entry deck and bay. The top floor is given over to the master bedroom suite. Massive closet (right), bath (left), and central non-view-oriented sleeping space all sit in the central long bay of the house, defined by the flat roof above its location in the plan. Note the double-height convection spaces flanking the space above the central deck, and the strategic skylight locations aiding local axes and providing illumination at the oblique incidence of the shed roof to the third floor.*

5

bedroom suite, including a walk-in closet and a large bath. Skylights illuminate double-height spaces and special parts of the lofty master bedroom. The large-scale deck is appropriately sun worshiping, and the house is a model of passive solar techniques. Stairs, wood stove, and roofing patterns are overtly custom and contemporary in their outlook. In short, there are no pretensions of a romantically reminiscent house beyond the raw directness of the formal dynamics.

In creating an axial entry, double-height spatial flow, and an unrestrained vantage from which to possess the Colorado countryside, Lipsey has evidenced a skill at making a small house lose its potential for self-pity in favor of the celebration of its situation.

By applying the innocently eccentric motifs of frontier architecture (with an occasional nautical allusion), Lipsey has added charm to a potentially blank, hillside-viewing platform. When the formal, spatial, and historical maneuvers are organized about the principles of passive solar heating and the considered efforts to effect functional efficiency, a delightful small house results.

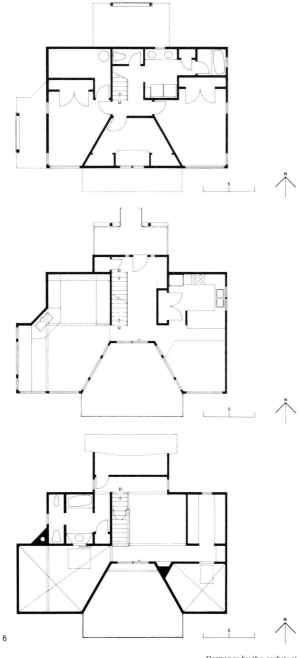

6

Drawings by the architect

Speculative Adventure

Mark Simon takes on the challenge of designing a house within elusive programmatic guidelines.

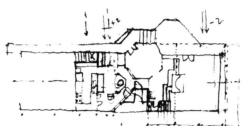

Mark Simon was asked by a national magazine to design a speculative house (built to be sold) for its readership. It's flattering to be chosen for such a task, but it's not easy to design for no one in particular. To be actively engaged in the design of a house for the prototypical American family can be quite frustrating when that family exists only on paper.

Of course, Simon could have simply napkin-sketched his way through the project, effecting a novel, two-dimensionally evocative building that may or may not have been livable architecture. But as a true professional, Simon executed the job with such skill that the results are far better than what might have been expected given the nature of the task undertaken.

Mark Simon treated his design as a laboratory for both his particular thoughts about aesthetics and his theories on passive solar techniques. Of course any spec house has a stringent budget, and Simon wanted to maximize his design's impact for the dollar. In that spirit, he implemented many of the guidelines advocated in the introduction of this book.

Many of these elements that make small houses more livable make houses more profitable. The sense of space, the quality of surprise, the differentiation of scale, the use of the vertical dimension, all of these principles add greatly to the amenity of a house without greatly increasing the cost of construction.

It is in the level of finish and in the quality of detailing that a spec house suffers from the profit motive. Rather than reinventing certain aspects of a home to personalize its appeal and enhance its utility, developers of spec houses will assemble brand-name catalog components to create a menu of desirable parts

ARCHITECT'S STATEMENT

Designed to be a passive solar house, the New England hillside home recalls those of the Berkshire Mountains. It sits on a simple foundation—20 feet wide × 80 feet long—which makes it economical to build, and it is oriented to the south, which makes it economical to heat. At the same time, its roof line and stained red cedar shingle siding enliven the design. With deep overhangs and trellises, expansive windows, and oversize chimneys, the house looks like a mansion, much larger than its 2200 square feet.

Because the house has a majority of its windows facing south and has roof overhangs or trellises to shade the windows during the summer, its design is especially energy-efficient. Combining that with historical imagery and simple construction, this home pioneers new directions for modern American homes. Constructed of natural materials, it is affordable, comfortable, and durable.

Mark Simon

LIST OF PARTICULARS

Burlington house
Location: Burlington, Connecticut
Architect: Mark Simon, assisted by F. Bradford Drake
Budget: Not available
Nominal space: 2200 square feet
Perceived space: 2400 square feet

that convey a tangible value. Similarly, model homes are decorated to touch every trendy base on the cutting edge of gratuitously strident bric-a-brac. By dazzling glitz before the eyes of the average home buyer, a decorator can obscure the never-ending clamshell molding and the sloppy gypsum board work.

Given the low potential for customized design or quality finish work and given that his design would be used to display the latest taste in applied elements, Mark Simon set out to design a house of sufficient impact to assert its identity amid all the distractions.

Having chosen a site with good passive solar potential, the architect had the basic form predetermined in the now-classic rectangle elongated along the east-west axis to maximize the southerly exposure. Given the budgetary restrictions, no more than 2400 square feet could be built. And since the average young household has 3½ family members, 2½ bedrooms were required along with the subsequently obligatory 2½ baths and 2-car garage. Additionally the now-clichéd eat-in kitchen, family room, and social deck were requisites.

Two essential elaborations were effected upon the classic solar section form staked out by Simon. The first was external. Rather than deform the simple form of a solar-oriented rectangle, the architect gave this prototypical shell life by adding semidetached elements to the exterior. Stickwork, trelliswork, heavy overhangs, color staining, and a single grand dormer were applied to the undifferentiated oblong form. From the street side (which is south), the net result is to create a "head," or weighted end. The effective image is of a steamboat, locomotive, or leviathan cruising along the landscape.

All photos and drawings courtesy of the architect

Figure 1 *South, street side. With the garage to the left forming the "tail," progressively sized and spaced glazing culminates in the dominant dormer and extended double-hipped roof (right), which form the "head." Trellis (center), eave overhangs, and stickwork add a sense of depth to an otherwise potentially flat massing. Note the use of stained shingles as in-fill between sections of the upper window band, reinforcing its linear progression. Note how the stairway's diagonal influence translates this band to a first-floor level at the living room (right).*

Figure 2 *Stickwork. Applied timbers provide a rich skeletal ornament to the otherwise stark house form and also support heavy overhangs at dormer and living room.*

Figure 3 *North end. Living room access (left) is embraced by overhang wrapping around from the east end, while a double-height window (center) conveys a two-story space beyond as the bay window extension of the internal octagonal tower form swells forth. Beneath all these undulations extends the deck, bowed to create a space centered on the double-height window described.*

2

3

4

5

Figure 4 *Living room. Stair, chimney, and distant dining room present a complex vision of multiple harmonies. The stair is married to the southerly glazing under the massive dormer (note the use of a stock sliding glass door as a venting window below the fixed triangular lights). The massive fireplace form stands in counterpoint to the expressive void, catching and reflecting its light. To the right, a civilized dining room sits at a lower level, placidly bypassing the expressively large-scale elements described. Note the stickwork knee brace supporting the massive overhang to the upper left.*

Figure 5 *Interstitial interaction. A second-floor overlook (left) faces the back of the chimney (right), while the octagonal tower form (center) quietly bulges forth. The double-height window in right center background provides ventilation and backlighting.*

Figure 6 *Dining room. Set amid chimney, stair, and living room beyond, this spatial oasis, octagonal in plan, provides a centered space among all the animated parts. Note the expressive stepping fairly oozing toward this space.*

Figure 7 *Plans. A shallow bay provides deep solar penetration and formal impact from the street, while its potentially constricting width (20 feet) is mitigated by the imposition of considered elements such as fireplace, octagonal tower, space-extending deck, and raised, double-height living room. Aside from these focal points, the plan is kept quite simple, providing affordability and maximum utilization of available space.*

6

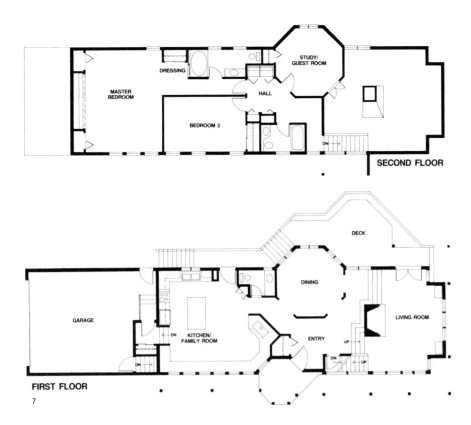

SECOND FLOOR

FIRST FLOOR

7

Internally the methods employed are similarly kinetic. Rather than design in a level of detail which would be both prohibitive in terms of cost and too competitive with the decoration that was to be applied, Mark Simon chose several large-scale plan elements and reinforced their relative importance while soft-pedaling other parts. The focal points include the stair, the living space, and an internal tower of dining room below and study above.

A graduated formality can be seen on the first floor: from the westerly garage, to the kitchen, to the entry and dining room, and finally to the grand living space facing east. Upstairs there is a similar progression: from the thoroughly private easterly master bedroom, to the children's bedroom, to the guest room–study, and finally to the highly visible clerestory space above the living area facing west. The wall surfaces of all these spaces are covered in painted Sheetrock. It is in such coordinated layerings that an architect knits his or her intentions into a spatial fabric of reinforcing organization.

Apart from the applied elements described, the exterior of the house is essentially a broad wall of shingles punctuated by windows in a progressive pattern and capped with a steeply pitched roof covered in asphalt shingles.

The consistency of surface treatments inside and out allows the application of overtly distinct parts to occur without confusion or internal competition.

There are three areas where internal and external elements coalesce to provide a degree of formal and spatial interplay. First, and most obvious, is the interior octagonal tower of bedroom and study, which is allowed to bulge through the otherwise continuous north wall membrane in the form of a bay window. Second, the double-height living room space allows for a double-hipped roof end above. Last, and most important, the aforementioned grand gable is integral to the interior stair; the diagonal line of its angle is effected in the bottom edge of the glazing pattern that fills the dormer face. The stair is the main convection space, and its glazing serves as the only overt void in the facade, all other fenestration being standard casement windows, banded but distinctly framed.

By organizing standard components and materials in an animated manner, Simon evidences how an architect can create amenity and hence value without increasing building cost. By applying simple, aggrandizing, ornamental tack-ons, Simon provides a thoroughly customized image for a relatively low cost.

Extraordinary Augmentation

Alex Camayd destroys the limits of his own house via window dressing in the grandest of terms.

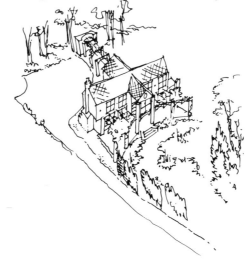

Occupancy of a house can be a matter of primitive spatial harbor or an elaboration upon human utility to the point of thorough accommodation. Similarly, a small house can be a shack or the expressed potential of its latent organizing parts.

The house Alex Camayd designed for himself and his wife, Nan Camayd, is 300 square feet larger than the nominal criteria of 2000 square feet for a two-bedroom house that was used to select projects for this book. However, the perceived space of 3600 square feet is fully 50 percent larger than the nominal figure quoted. Given the extraordinary perceptual impact this house has on those encountering it, it is well worth discussion as an example of the methods that can be employed to defeat the potential limits of any house.

The classic issues of public and private orientation, axial organization, encounter and procession, scalar variety, energy efficiency, and defined versus enclosed space are all creatively and elegantly addressed by this project.

The Camayds purchased a partially cleared lot facing a marvelous exterior space sitting on the edge of a hill. The architect-owner immediately saw the potential for the house to be situated as both a wall against and an access to the defined exterior space.

To order the access, extraordinary axial orientations made great sense if large-scale ordinates were to be addressed. The problem was that such large-scale axes could virtually dwarf the actual house. The solution was to give the initial encountering axis a subdominant cross axis. Because the ordinates of this axis were due east and west, a perfect solar orientation was effected.

ARCHITECT'S STATEMENT

In planning our new home, my wife, Nan, and I sought to achieve a personal expression of our own aesthetic values in a suburban neighborhood of conventional houses. Our property offered the possibility of an extroverted design as well as a high degree of privacy.

Free from the relationship to the street, one enters the house from the stoic north elevation and proceeds through a foyer flanked by a colonnade that cuts through and extends beyond the house to embrace, with its sweeping arms, the garden beyond. Other spaces become incidental to this path.

Serving as both the architect and general contractor during the construction of the home, I discovered how difficult and sometimes frustrating it can be to balance these roles. However, this means Nan and I were able to retain careful control of the project and could work closely with the local craftsmen who produced many custom-designed details for the house.

Alex Camayd

LIST OF PARTICULARS

Camayd house
Location: Clarks Summit,
　Pennsylvania
Architect: Alex Camayd
Budget: $130,000
Nominal space: 2300 square feet
Perceived space: 3600 square feet

If these organizational spines were simply allowed to interface crudely as east-west house mass colliding with north-south entry vista, then there would be little to write about. It is the elaborations upon preconception that add delight and utility to any house design. With their house set amid a rather unexceptional array of typical American suburban homes, the Camayds recognized the opportunity to create a minor-league major landmark.

The budget was indeed tight for a home with honest aspirations toward grandeur, so ingenuity was implemented with a vengeance.

A simple-span, two-story, extruded-gable form is violated by a two-story grand hall–entrance at its midpoint. Asymmetrical functional accommodations defuse the potentially dictatorial scale and add a touch of light eccentricity to the facade detailing. To the south an interior colonnade receiving the entry axis extends to a lofty portico and then laterally extends to form an arcing array of freestanding columns addressing the major exterior space.

The house itself is simply a wall that is penetrated by the axis, punctuated by windows, and used as a formal datum for the bowed array of columns facing the open south prospect. Compositional and material consistencies convey a designed ensemble of expressive parts. Squares of enormous scalar differentiation—from 8 inches to 6 feet—form the window and door openings. Cylindrical columns sans base, capital, or entasis provide support, form axes and cross axes, and stand as formal ornament. Stucco serves as a plastic covering of all exterior surfaces.

Perhaps the most impressive tool of design consistently implemented by

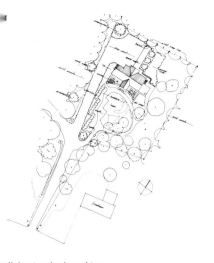

Figure 1 *Site. With the house-form axis set at the minor cross ordinate, the major aligning orientation is derived from the initial point of apprehension, the corner of Highland Avenue (bottom). Fortunately the orientation also allows for optimum solar gain.*

Figure 2 *Southeast. A simple extended-gable form is used as a wall off which large-scale appliqués can assert themselves and aggrandize the house form. Proud portico, embracing colonnade, private deck extension (right)—all utilizing semiornamental latticework—are covered in the same stucco as the main house, and all save the pointed vertical (right) are formed to be abstracted objects, unprecedented in the house exterior.*

All drawings by the architect

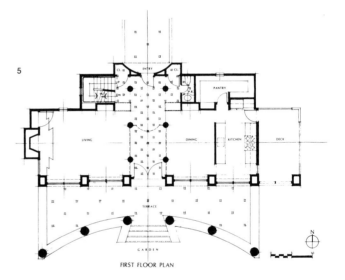

5

FIRST FLOOR PLAN

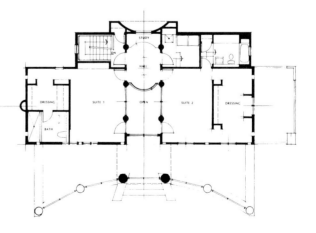

SECOND FLOOR PLAN

Figure 3 *South, centered axis. Square window and door openings range in size from inches to feet. Relentlessly immutable symmetry is avoided by the occasional eccentricity of a window (upper left) or the casting off of a special element (lower right). Note the levitated pediment above the abstracted columns.*

Figure 4 *Internal axis. Facing south, the major site and entry orientation divides bedroom suites (above) and dining room (left) from living room (right). Custom doors, floor pattern, and lofted portico above all respond to this focal space. Note the use of color and of obscuring sandblasted glass panels infilling about columns on the second floor.*

Figure 5 *Plans. Note that in both plans all service spaces are relegated to the entry side (upper part of plan) in the form of a minor bay set asymmetrically to the house form. The first-floor areas (top) of living room, dining room, kitchen, and deck extension make up an extremely large-scale domestic space, whose impact is strengthened by the full-width glazing, axial orientations, and perceived extension of the space to the arcing colonnade to the south. Entry itself is oriented to the axis defined by the internal columns, the floor pattern, the tangent point of the colonnade curve, the two-story interior space, and the bowed overlook from the second floor. The second floor (bottom) uses this axis to divide the two bedroom suites.*

Camayd is not a material, geometry, or physical element but rather a specific type of spatial definition. An outdoor "room," as utilized by Camayd, is not simply a deck, patio, or porch. Camayd's outdoor rooms are both thoroughly defined (by ground surface treatment, edge definition, and sometimes roof coverage) and civilized (by detailing and integration with the interior). The interstitial zone between the south facade and the bowed row of freestanding columns presents a spatial definition that is at once sophisticated and powerful. The overtly flat south wall with multiple-scale openings stands quite proudly in definitive solidity as a foil to the animated and abstracted column array. Secondarily, an informal deck to the east extends the plane of the south wall beyond enclosed space.

By utilizing mansion-scaled elements within the context of a diminutive house, Camayd has used the axial order and abstracted formal identities to control the composed spaces and parts.

A similar expansive elegance is carried on through the interior of the house. The double-height entry hall is defined by its height and colonnade but has its space shared by the massive living-dining room. The openness is enhanced by the use of a decorative partition screening the kitchen from view while allowing wall and ceiling planes to remain uninterrupted. The perceived space is 50 feet long and 20 feet wide, a scale that defines the true size of the house. This extraordinary openness is further enhanced by glazed in-fill along the entire length of the 50-foot south wall. Because the living-dining room opens up to one of the aforementioned outdoor rooms, which is defined by the column array, the impact of the space is virtually doubled. Another factor increasing the sense of space is the ceiling height, which breaks the normal 8-foot limit by over a foot. Obviously some functional organization helped create this monumental domestic space; all ancillary spaces of bath, pantry, closet, stair, and vestibule are relegated to a deep-wall subbay to the north.

On the second floor, which is open to view from the entry hall through sandblasted glass screens, two generous bedroom suites flank the major axis intrusion through the house.

Prioritizing unlimited spatial revelry on such a scale is unprecedented in this book. If all that was attempted was a greedy agglomeration of space, then there would be an empty presence of elegant air. But Camayd has used a variety of textures, colors, and elements to subdivide space and add a scale that rewards close inspection.

How can so much perceived space, compositional whimsy, and custom detailing be afforded? Apart from the applied parts of colonnade, ornamental rails, and surface treatments, the form of the house itself is thoroughly mundane. A plain extruded-gable form is allowed to be decorated by cleverly orchestrated voids and enlivening columns, porticoes, and outdoor rooms. The impact of this house is thus greatly enhanced, and its level of intention and realization is vastly extended.

Alex Camayd has displayed the prioritized organization, formal ingenuity, and creative detailing that allow any size house to live in our consciousness beyond its physical limitations. In his liberated posture as owner-architect, he has taken up the challenge of a wonderful site and has created a positive statement of unique impact.

Alex Camayd

Alex Camayd

Figure 6 *Living room. The view is oriented to the centerline of the fireplace and the aligning columns. The scale of the large first-story space can be perceived as the fireplace seems quite distant; note the use of the mirror (right) to further extend space. Note also the curved overlook into the two-story space between the columns (upper right).*

Figure 7 *Dining room. With the kitchen beyond obscured by the screen wall, the actual limits to the space—walls and ceiling—are allowed to bypass this spatial delineation. Note the height of the ceiling and the heavy curtains on the southerly glazing, which are utilized to prevent summer overheating and winter radiant cooling at night.*

A Town House Revisited

Thompson E. Penney designs his own house in a refreshing revision of traditional Charleston architecture.

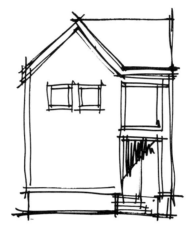

The empowerment of an architect designing his or her own home often results in an artistic frenzy only tempered by a parsimonious budget. When confronted with the opportunity to design his own home, Thompson E. Penney, a Charleston, South Carolina, architect, opted for a rousing re-creation rather than a rowdy aesthetic experiment.

The American south has one of the few nonhomogenized cultures left in the United States. Architecture of the last 3 centuries accommodated the heat, the plantation, the Civil War, and the cotton business. Shade-producing overhangs and foliage, breeze-oriented openings, and endless verandas helped beat the heat, while symmetry, grand staircases, columns, and wrought-iron detailing were the tip of the aesthetic iceberg explored by southern architects.

The very nature of twentieth-century architecture is rejectionist. Past idiosyncrasies, foibles, and traditions have all been rejected at one time or another in the twentieth century. Even environmental accommodation was ignored by architects of the middle third of this century in favor of an assumed timelessly universal aesthetic. Architectural Esperanto was intended to create a new, borderless world. The passage of time has revealed that the desire to redefine all the theories and practices of building design was the product of rampaging egos rather than selfless humanism. The product of this futurist aesthetic is some of the most dated and foolish architecture ever built.

To run against the current of millenia of experience and thought may be heroic, but it is also a bit absurd. The notion that there is a closed aesthetic door behind each "new" building begs for disastrous errors of inexperience.

ARCHITECT'S STATEMENT

The problem of capturing the spirit of the past without compromising the principles and pressures that should shape contemporary design is a classic one. Although the site for the house was located in an outlying area of Charleston, South Carolina, designated by the developer as a version of a historic Charleston neighborhood, the program rejected the popular convention of assembling typical elements and details in a caricature of traditional architecture. Instead the approach was to seek those physical and philosophical characteristics of the eighteenth- and nineteenth-century Charleston house that are valid responses in our time and to interpret these in a contemporary building.

As with form, the traditional has not been allowed to dictate a choice of materials and details. Rather, the archetype has been used as a tool for discovery, to suggest and confirm those responses that are reasonable for any time in one place and that constitute a true connection with the past.

Thompson E. Penney

LIST OF PARTICULARS

The Penney house
(Contemporary Charleston Single House 1)
Location: Charleston, South Carolina
Architect: Thompson E. Penney
Budget: $48,000 (1980)
Nominal space: 2400 square feet
Perceived space: 3200 square feet

Penney saw these errors in his hometown. He also divined a consistent tradition of town-house design that was indeed charming in its antiquity but also sensible. To simply photocopy his favorite extant town house would bypass all the tools Penney could bring to bear on the problem. The application of new technologies, the rethinking of the identities of building components, and the accommodation of a contemporary way of life personalized to the home owner are the fundamental motivators for all progress in architecture (including the Modern Movement). So with a working palette of interpretive consistencies with the architecture that surrounded his site, Penney applied his creative spirit to effect a striking small house.

His urban lot, elongated and tight to the street, and his program, to accommodate a family of three or four people, were prototypical.

His response is a prototype of contextualism as applied to small-house design. The 16-foot-wide, 82-foot-long house occupies less than 25 percent of the lot area, while it visually dominates the immediate surroundings. The long form is internally subdivided—both structurally and functionally—into four bays and has a semidetached stair held distinct from the south face. The stair is the dominant part of an 8-foot-wide subbay that runs the full length of the house and also includes the entry and two decks. Each of these four elements relates to one of the four subbays of the house itself. The duets of two aligned spaces each cause cross-axial orientation against the force and focus of the elongated house form. Essentially, from west to east the four bays are the studio, which overlooks the entry deck and steps, the kitchen, which

1

All photos by Gordon H. Schenck, Jr.

Figure 1 *West, street. This is a proud elevation derived from traditional Charleston town-house facades. The focused glare of the eyeball window gaze is facilitated by the absence of first-story windows below. The traditional porch has been distilled into a simple perforated extension of the clapboard exterior (right). Note the hidden gutters and minimal overhangs and the absence of ornament—all conspiring to objectify this familiar house form.*

Figure 2 *Contextual source. These Charleston town houses served as the parental influence to Penney's creation.*

Figure 3 *South facade, at night. This view shows that the public-space glazing (right) is merely the strip application of the voids formed by the megalattice (left). Such overt consistency engenders a sense of complete design, giving a composed quality to the house form. Note that the dramatic backlighting of the entry court is implemented by the use of two standard, surface-mount flood lamps. The raked roof of the stair can be seen to be merely a vaulting leap of the cornice datum carried around the house by the entry lattice. Note also the continuity of all clapboard lines.*

Figure 4 *The Megalattice. Formed by a simple extension of the house's clapboard skin and excision of the square openings defined by the clapboard spacing lines, this huge-scale element both defines an entry court and extends the perceived scale of the house. Note how the integral gutters, eave vents, and minimal overhangs conspire with a dearth of ornament to further convey a sense of scale-ambiguous objectification. Note also the incised entry at center bottom.*

2

3

4

Figure 5 *Site axonometric. This shows the fully realized site development of "ground facades" (actually, paved areas for cars and inhabitants) to the south. The house form is shown to be a simple extruded-gable form with applied parts of decks, megalattice, and stair to the south increasing its impact. The very smallness of the footprint of the house itself lends a great deal of amenity to the house situation.*

Figure 6 *Living and dining spaces. Open and yet defined by the dropped beam (above) and dropped floor plane, these two spaces are the main internal volumes presented in the house. The horizontal flow stands in stark contrast to the vertical focus of the entry facade and southern entry court. Note also that the ambiguity of modernity used on the entry form is given up in this thoroughly contemporary space.*

Figure 7 *Stairs. Serving as light well, hot-air flue, and vertical spatial release, this space is overtly a transitional gesture between floors given the plasticity of the rail form and the objectified inner wall (center) set at the juncture of the two floors.*

Figure 8 *Master bedroom, entry. The only integral two-story space in the house (as opposed to the applied stair tower), this minor balcony allows air and light to flow but constricts view into the bedroom. Note that this is the peekaboo vantage from which the space is obliquely apprehended but that actual entry is reserved for a cross-axial corridor to the right of the picture presented, behind the bed.*

Figure 9 *Master bedroom. Multiple meanings are revealed in this photo, as the balcony rail is shown to be a bookcase; and the bed headboard, the back of a closet. Note the air-return grate at the corner and the vaulted ceiling treatment.*

5

AXONOMETRIC
CCSH 1

All drawings by the architect

6

7

8

9

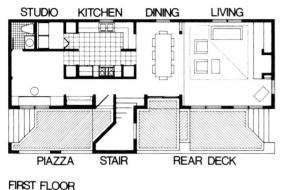

STUDIO   KITCHEN   DINING   LIVING

PIAZZA   STAIR   REAR DECK

FIRST FLOOR

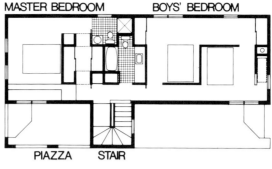

MASTER BEDROOM   BOYS' BEDROOM

PIAZZA   STAIR

SECOND FLOOR

Figure 10 *Plans. Essentially, an extruded, narrow bay is subdivided in the short direction into four bays and has a secondary narrow bay applied to its length for ancillary exterior spaces and stair. Two full-length axes run the entire length of the house along the south wall on both floors. All wet functions occur in the lower middle bay, isolating the master bedroom and study suite.*

encounters the stair and front door, the dining area, which has a deck opposite, and the sunken living room, which also has a deck opposite, with backyard-accessing steps.

Vertically, the organization places the master bedroom above the studio, two baths above the kitchen, and a double children's bedroom above the dining-living half of the house.

With stair and wet functions aligned, a nice isolation of the west-end master bedroom and studio is effected, creating a semisuite. In this way the narrow house form enhances separation and creates a sense of space—underscored by a tiny two-story spatial linkage along the south wall.

To counterpoint the traditional aspects of massing—southern orientation of facade elements and exterior spaces along the subbay described—Penney has used overtly contemporary detailing (white gypsum walls, deemphasized trim, rectilinear windows and walls, etc.) and a fresh plan organization to breathe new life and his personal predilections into this house. Some of the interesting elements he has inserted include a clear major axis along the entire south wall of the first and second floors, a large, double children's bedroom with mutually exclusive division of space created through thorough separation of orientation within one room, and a small two-story space at the entry, which is oriented to the master bedroom and which serves as a barrier to immediate access but a release to the axis mentioned.

The exterior also conveys the sense of revised tradition. The narrow-ended home with flanking bay of outside-oriented spaces and entry is quite traditional to the area. A symmetrical gable end on the main house form at the street and a subdominant flat roof form on the subbay are also prototypical of the housing genre around and about Penney's site. Penney used these elements but starkly objectified some and exaggerated others to the point where there is no doubting that this is a new house form devoid of rationalizations or compromises.

The most obviously deviant expression of recreated tradition is the street-end facade. Here Penney creates distilled sculpture from the elements he reinvents. The gable end, symmetrical and proud, is reduced to a blank outline facade, perforated by only two square "eyeball" windows at the second story (opposite each master bedroom inhabitant). The subbay, traditionally a multipiece-veranda extravaganza, becomes a simple wraparound extension of the gable facade materials; clapboard and eave lines extend in a two-story "megalattice," open at the top. The defined space is described by Penney as a piazza. Essentially, six square openings are cut into the clapboard fabric, with all surfaces painted white and with absolutely no decorative detailing. Entry is thus framed, and the first southern subspace is defined.

The second reinvention, the remote peninsular stair (normally buried within the house form), completes the front facade confrontation with the street. It, too, is blankly wrapped in the clapboard fabric, maintaining its eave height and clapboard lines with the main house form. The front door sits within a carved-out niche of the stair monolith. The exterior form of the stair, like the house itself, initially conveys subjugation to the traditional (roof pitch, eave height, clapboard wrap), but as you penetrate the site, the seemingly standard roof is shown to be a rakish shed roof formed by one-half of the main house's gable roof form.

Windows, or the absence of windows, create a modernized sensibility as well. When used in this house, they are either simple squares or combinations of squares, devoid of muntins. At entry and stair a desire for privacy has caused the elimination of windows altogether, giving the clapboard skin further expressive planes to occupy.

The familiar dances with the surprising, and this small house gains stature through a traditional extension of impact gained with the use of aggrandizing, tacked-on elements of entry walls, stair, and decks. When these are combined with the refreshing plan elements utilized by Thompson E. Penney, the result is a marvelous mesh of domestic tranquillity and modern messages.

Invigorating Burial

Jersey Devil designs and builds an extraordinary work of inhabitable art in California.

© 1969 Ed Sheetz

Antonio Gaudi was an architect who created fantastic structures in the first half of this century. His name is synonymous with the Art Nouveau aesthetic of curvilinear flow and organic form. His designs evoke a sense of uncontrolled permutation creating architectural organisms of self-sustaining growth. Given his work, one might assume that the oozing, gooey flow of form and space was designed by an artist of limited technical insight. In truth, Gaudi was trained as an engineer, and his designs were subjected to thorough structural analysis by the use of large-scale models.

The parallels between Antonio Gaudi, master of organic architecture in early-twentieth-century Spain, and Jersey Devil, an itinerant group of design-and-build architect-contractors based in New Jersey, are many and mutually enhancing.

The image of a highly engineered, technologically sophisticated, and structurally innovative building is not implicitly organic. Just as Gaudi presented buildings that obscured their thoroughly considered structural design, Jersey Devil has created a house of a thoroughly organic sensibility that conceals rigorous technical analysis and fundamental innovations in structural engineering. The house design responds to the unique hilltop site by solar orientation and wind-deflecting formal design. But the single most impressive feature of this house design is its buried form, with sod roof, excavated entry court, and cave-style garage.

The owners, a family of five, knew what they were getting into when they contacted Steve Badanes and Jim Adamson of Jersey Devil. They possessed a unique piece of land with a spectacular view and desired a home to meet the challenge of the wind-swept site.

ARCHITECT'S STATEMENT

The house is cut into the crest of the hill to present a low profile to storm winds. Digging the structure into a south "bowl" deflects wind over the building while still allowing for sun penetration (the curved shape also pushes wind around it). Following the contours of the ridge, the house creates a protected exterior space by wrapping around a "sunken" courtyard.

The use of earth berms, natural stone veneer, retaining walls, and a sod roof literally blends the house with its awesome site (per planning-board requirements).

Living in a passive solar house has changed the owners' living patterns so that they have become more aware of their microclimate.

The side that faces nature (ocean, sun, wind) is clearly synthetic, hard-edged and technology-oriented. The side which faces "civilization" (Silicon Valley) is free-flowing, organic, and lushly landscaped. Fantasy and image come into play as the house seeks to transcend the "solar-diagram" approach.

Steve Badanes

LIST OF PARTICULARS

Hill House
Location: La Honda, California
Architects: Jersey Devil, Steve Badanes and Jim Adamson presiding
Budget: $242,000 (1979)
Nominal space: 2460 square feet
Perceived space: 3100 square feet

The photographs convey the unrestrained flow of the house's form, space, and elements. The consistent curvilinear articulation of so many components stands in joyous contrast to the popular image of a "nouveau-techno" house. It would be easy to assume that a group of young aesthetes tromping about the country designing and fabricating admittedly bizarre buildings is more interested in style than content. But nothing could be further from the truth. This home design is thoroughly keyed to utility and harmony with an extraordinary site.

Jersey Devil provided the owners with a home that destroys the preconceptions engrained in the popular consciousness of the typical bermed, or buried, solar house. There are no visible raw-concrete walls, no tacked-on or prefabricated greenhouses or solar panels. The house has no awkwardly lumped mounding about its form clumsily concealing a less than innovative house plan cosmetically covered with a few feet of dirt.

Buried-home practitioners continuously cry out that there are no sacrifices in building an earth-sheltered house, and many advantages. But putting dirt on your roof, digging your bedroom into a hillside, and viewing the world from a singular vantage point have obvious consequences beyond the simple energy savings provided by the high insulating value of earth. The earth used to cover these homes is not like asphalt shingles or concrete. Dirt does not tolerate rectilinear order. It erodes. It settles. It sprouts thoroughly chaotic vegetation.

Rather than try to tame the earth and rewrite the laws of nature, Jersey Devil used the very mutability of the dirt employed to generate a buried home that celebrates its hilltop posture.

1

Figure 1 *South. A curving wall of glass above and glazing over Trombe wall below slices the terrain. Note the naked posture of the situation.*

Figure 2 *North. There is a dynamic interweaving of sod-covered house form and insinuating gravel access. The fulcrum of all the curving permutation is the circular court nestled under the arm of earth that is the house. Note the stingray extension of the roof to the center point of the court radius. Note also the cave-cum-garage (center left).*

Figure 3 *The court view. As organic as the landscape it is embraced within, this seeming excision is in truth a court defined by the back of the applied house (left). The floating roof form extends a pseudopod to touch the earth and spawn a planter. A sympathetic hot tub sits amid an ooze of decking. Rocks form walls and sculpture and provide support. Note that all of these geometries are radially defined and are not simply meanderingly gratuitous in generation.*

2

3

4

Mikkel Aaland

Figure 4 *Entry. Harbored beneath the descending roof extension, the front door (right) is a simple void in the rock-faced wall that defines the back of the house. Custom windows (center) provide backlighting and ventilation.*

Figure 5 *Hot tub. Spawned by the planter beyond, this California necessity is marvelously embraced by the courtyard. Note minideck, also circular, nestled against the raw-rock wall.*

Figure 6 *Plan. A rectangular plan is bent at one end to effect a simple quarter radius. Entry occurs at the west end of the living area, forming a cross axis to the central circulation spine running the entire length of the house. Note how this entry axis is extended by the peninsular deck radially cast off the south facade. The major longitudinal axis separates northern serving spaces from the bedrooms to the southeast and extends to form the entry of the master bedroom suite to the southwest. The northerly courtyard defined by the quarter twist of the plan has its full circular potential effected by the extension of the flanking east and west earth berms to form a thoroughly protected exterior space.*

5

This very special case uniquely tests the small-house theories described in the introduction of this book. Jersey Devil has used earth-sheltered and passive solar techniques with an extraordinary degree of sophistication and sensitive expression to create a four-bedroom, 2460-square-foot home. The sense of constricted square footage was not the only design aspect that had to be defeated. With any earth-sheltered house, the very act of burial puts severe height restrictions on any interior spaces set beneath sod.

Internally, Jersey Devil used the surprise engendered in curvilinear organization, the release of full-width glazing, and axial orientations that provide spatial linkage to effect a small house with a grand posture. On the exterior, defined but unenclosed spaces were used to functionally liberate and perceptually expand the house. Additionally, overtly expressive elements were extruded from the house form to expand its impact on the site—a twist on the form of window dressing that has helped aggrandize buildings throughout history.

In plan, the seemingly convoluted form is revealed to be nothing more than an extended, shallow-section rectangle bent at one end to a quarter radius. The house is entered through the court formed about the center point of the radius. A cross axis releases the visitor upon entry.

The elongated form orients all noninhabited service spaces to the north side and locates three bedrooms, the family-guest room, the living area, and the study along the longer building side of the house form. Between the serving spaces and the served southerly spaces, a continuous axis of circulation runs through the entire house from east garage to west master bedroom suite.

Obviously this house was not built with a severely limited budget, but several major economies were effected that have much merit. First, the builders were also the designers. The empowerment of directly expressed creativity facilitates the normal flow of ideas to and from the designer and the builder, saving time and money. Second, the aggressive use of solar gain in the form of a Trombe wall heat sink and southerly orientation, when combined with the extraordinary insulating value of bermed construction, generates enormous energy savings. The owners rarely if ever use their backup heating system. Last, and most discreetly, the house form gives an ingenious illusion of burial, when in truth a simple structure spans between two mounds of earth and is then covered with dirt. By using a bridge to extend a sod overlay, Jersey Devil built lightly upon the land while seemingly insinuating the house structure into the very bowels of the earth.

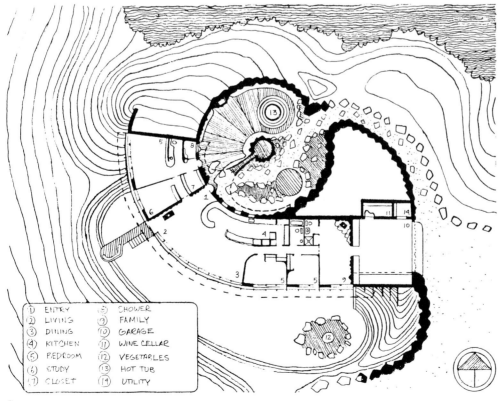

① ENTRY	⑧ SHOWER
② LIVING	⑨ FAMILY
③ DINING	⑩ GARAGE
④ KITCHEN	⑪ WINE CELLAR
⑤ BEDROOM	⑫ VEGETABLES
⑥ STUDY	⑬ HOT TUB
⑦ CLOSET	⑭ UTILITY

6

7

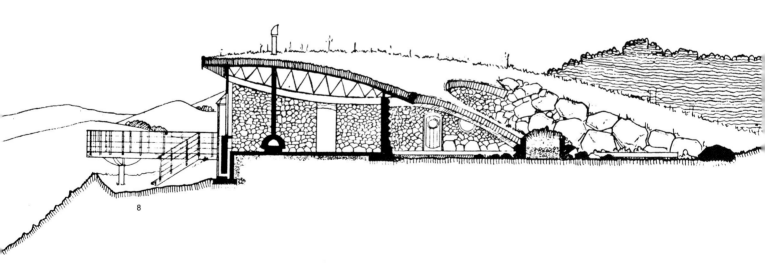

8

The innovative creativity of the essential construction is echoed in numerous details throughout the house. Two large-scale elements are in and of themselves quite impressive.

First, the Trombe wall mentioned evidences a resolution of a classic architectural paradox. Trombe walls are used to store heat. Heat is derived from the sun. The sun is only present when an unobstructed vantage can be secured. An unobstructed vantage facilitates a marvelous sense of spatial release, interior daylighting, and positive posturing toward a view—unless a thoroughly opaque wall gets in the way. In the competitive jockeying for the sun's undivided attention, the Trombe wall and the human eye have fought a battle that has had no winner, the compromise of either vested interest being a manifest failure.

The Hill House solves this quandary with a lowered Trombe wall, set below the normal windowsill height and held distinct from the foundation wall. The glazing that extends below the floor line gives adequate surface area for acceptable solar gain, and does so without imposing on the sweeping southern vista.

Earth-sheltered homes have two inherent problems: supporting the added dead load of dirt and providing adequate drainage without subsequent erosion. These two problems result from a radical design posture that often uses short-span roof framing, which cruelly subdivides interior space, or lowered ceiling heights, which dim spaces already dim enough because of their single exposure to the light of day.

Jersey Devil's solution brings us to the second highly creative large-scale element, which is both technically efficient and aesthetically rewarding. The heavy loads are collected in long-span, deep-web, double-bow trusses set at frequent intervals. The trusses are canted at an ascending angle, releasing the earth-topped space to the view and providing a gentle roof pitch to shed excess water that has no ground plane to drain into. Heavy loads are thus transferred to the closely spaced mullions of the south wall necessitated by its curvilinear form, and into the north wall, which is either earth-retaining or simply solid to avoid heat loss. All interior walls are nonbearing and are freed visually from the ceiling plane by Plexiglas glazing spanning to the exposed underside. The resulting space, ascendant with light captured by the bowed lower edge of the truss, is both exuberant and generated by the most prosaic of architectural needs: the need for a solid roof over the occupant's head.

The Hill House is fraught with creative detailing, more than likely designed on location as the designer-builders effected their reasoned fantasy.

Aesthetic spice is often added to standardized building systems to effect delight in uninspiring contexts. Often in the form of overt ornament, these applied elements of panache and style can be arbitrary and absurd. The Hill House, on the other hand, creates its own integral allure. The very nature of its dramatic posture atop a resplendent ridge demanded nothing less than a memorable building.

The architects of Jersey Devil have used their unique status as designers who build to evidence unvarnished aesthetic innovation in the context of uncompromising utility and technical sophistication. The worlds of prosaic use and artistic invention, so often held distinct, meld in this project to form a singularly stunning house.

Figure 7 *Living room. With ascending, bowed-truss ceiling, bowing southerly glazing, and stone-wall separation beyond, a richly detailed context is created, allowing curvilinear seating, counter, and bar to form subspaces within this open space. Innovation evidences itself as the glazing curves to meet the ceiling edge, the stone wall is held distinct from the truss underside, and the trusses themselves create a unique quality of suspension and depth.*

Figure 8 *Section. Facing west, the bowed truss is set at an angle to release the living room space and provide a slight pitch for dirt drainage above. Note how the southerly glazing extends beyond the line of support for the roof and finally becomes insulating sheathing for the floating Trombe wall set partially below the floor plane to allow uninterrupted visual release from within. Note the protected entry under the extended arch of the roof, an extension that touches the ground to form a planter at the center point of the house's major curve in plan.*

Little Big House

Laura Hartman and Richard Fernau create a little Italy in a house for a large family.

This is not the largest house in this book—but it certainly appears to be.

A family originally from Italy (Rome, to be precise) resettled in America's best imitation of a Roman climate, the wine-growing region north of San Francisco. It is not a home born of a meager budget, but it is indeed a model of maximized perceptual impact for a house of its genre.

It is significant that a home that might have been a distended agglommeration of spatial bloat, a house that has 4 bedrooms, 3½ baths, a 2-car garage, 6 discrete public spaces, 6 outdoor rooms, and 2 stairs, is all contained or defined by a relatively paltry 3100 square feet.

"Small" is indeed a relative adjective. A small football player is a huge jockey. This house of seemingly large proportions is really a modestly sized house of maximized formal impact.

This house was not designed merely to impress those who encounter it. Its linearity has more to do with creating structural support to parallel the slope of a difficult hillside site than with creating an architectural billboard.

Given the structurally beneficial linearity and the inherently complicated design program, this building easily could have been built as a typical California megastructure, an aircraft-carrier-meets-the-International-Style home designed more for effect than for human accommodation.

But the architects employed to create the design for this house were not content to simply abide by the slope, subdivide some modernist-slab building form, collect their check, and hit the hot tub; Richard Fernau and Laura Hartman are exquisitely revisionist. Rather than simply provide a single expressive house

ARCHITECTS' STATEMENT

The clients for the Maoli house are Roman, and the climate is Tuscan. Situated on the steep eastern slope of Lucas Valley, 30 miles north of San Francisco, the house is a collection of indoor and outdoor rooms strung along the contours.

The house is composed of a collection of discrete rooms, each with its own character while still belonging to the whole. The relationship between the house and the land is not a merger but a marriage of opposites, with a series of outdoor rooms mediating between the building and the landscape.

Despite its generous acreage, the site is restricted: two active slides define a building envelope into which the house is wedged. To save on foundation and site-development costs and to address the view to the east, the house runs north-south, parallel with the contours.

Fernau & Hartman

LIST OF PARTICULARS

Maoli house

Location: San Rafael, California

Architects: Fernau & Hartman

Budget: Not available

Nominal space: 3100 square feet

Perceived space: 4300 square feet

form, they combined a multitude of house forms to create an Italianate ensemble.

Somewhat akin to a Mediterranean village clustered precariously on a cliff-side harbor, or perhaps a monastery set high above society, or perhaps even an architectural family of pieces and parts in familial harmony while expressive of their distinctions, this house is fascinatingly enigmatic. A grand scale is effected of multiple houses, more irregular than a condominium but more linearly organized than a village. Yet the kinetic mass is also somehow monolithic in its abstracted freight train of stucco-covered form. The multiple impressions of Tuscan tenement, casual mansion, and simply a house that would not stop reproducing itself have an almost magical mystique.

As said, Fernau and Hartman have achieved this effect through carefully studied planning—focused effort that runs counter to the semi-ad-hoc aesthetic evidenced. It is only when the plans themselves are closely inspected that the layering of sequences, spaces, and forms becomes objectified.

Rather than give us a gratuitously rambling array of related but distinct components, Fernau and Hartman have effected a classic dynamic of internal counterpoint. One aesthete might call it a figure-ground paradox: Are the enclosed buildings or the defined outdoor spaces dominant? Another perspective is the datum-versus-dance harmony: Does the thoroughly rigid corridor linkage above and the sharp court edge below contain the formal expression or allow it to happen? Or is the plinth-and-corridor datum merely the Cartesian in dynamic tension with the organic kinetics of the various articulated forms? Endless theo-

1

Mark Citret

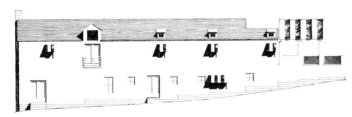

2

WEST ELEVATION
All drawings by the architects

3

EAST ELEVATION

Figure 1 *Distant prospect, east. A quiet agglomeration of forms and linkages, this house appears to be more of a village than a single-family home.*

Figure 2 *West elevation. A broad, flat plane punctuated by backlighting, cross-ventilating, hillside-facing windows.*

Figure 3 *East elevation. Each of the four bedrooms has an expressive gable form extending from the basic house form. Note the implicit directionality of the ongoing formal progression as the hill descends.*

Tim Street Porter

4

Figure 4 *Entry vista. With the look of an elevated "street in the air" or a multifamily project, the house has an undulating form that (left) defines exterior rooms. Note that each gable end is a bedroom.*

Figure 5 *Streetscape. Balconies spring forth from gables, which in turn bring forth columns. Note multidefined exterior rooms—defined either by interstitial position between gable extensions or by balconies overhead.*

Figure 6 *South, entry. The axially derived west datum eave line spawns gable extensions and shed dormers. Note the garage in the foreground ubiquitous stucco covering.*

Figure 7 *Corridor, axes. Tall shed dormers break roof underside and enliven a potentially superfocused space.*

5

Tim Street Porter

6

Lewis Watts

7

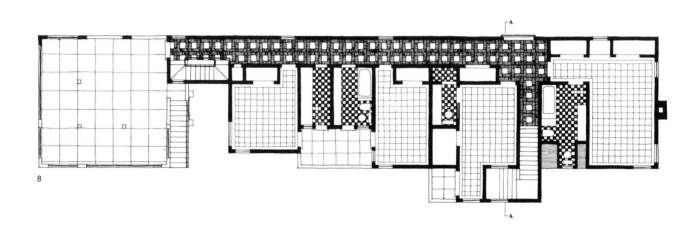

Gazebo   Bedroom   Laundry   Bath   Bedroom   Bedroom   Bath   Bedroom

8

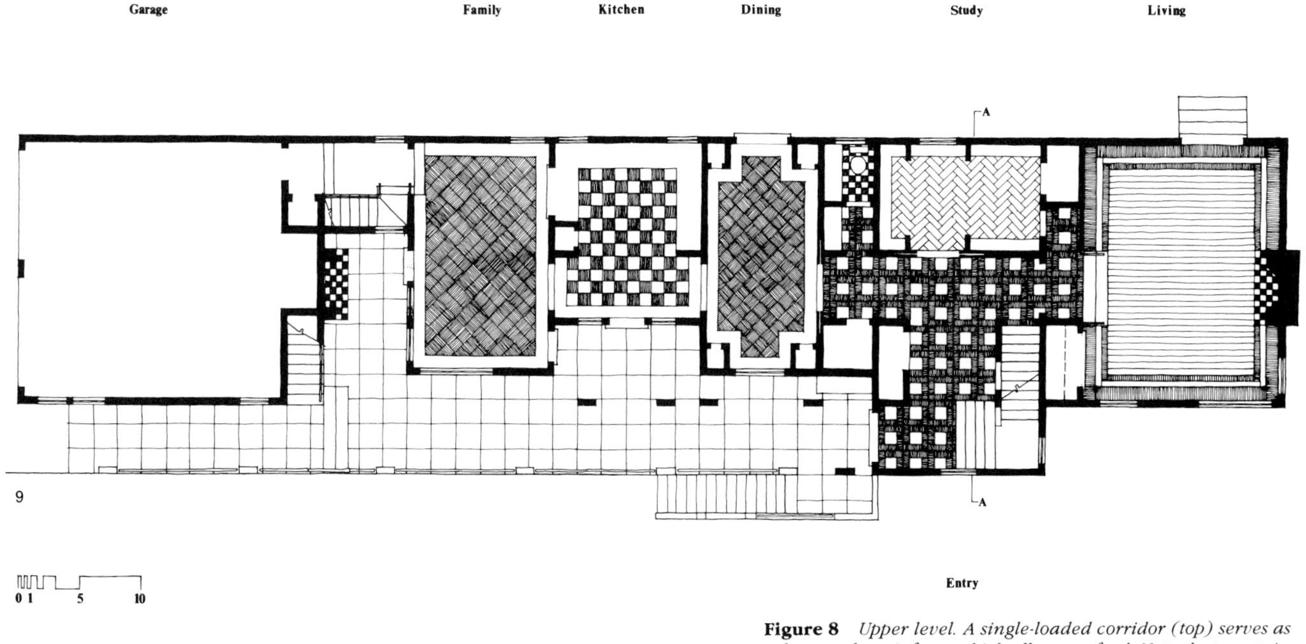

Garage   Family   Kitchen   Dining   Study   Living

9

0 1   5   10

Entry

Figure 8 *Upper level. A single-loaded corridor (top) serves as a long-scale axis from which all spaces feed. Note the two stairs, three baths, and three balconies, including the large-scale deck above the garage, which will accommodate a tent structure. Note also the repeated corner-window motif and use of closets as buffers.*

Figure 9 *Entry level. Floor patterns enhance the explicit distinctions between six separate public spaces. The entry has a grand spatial accommodation needed to turn the encountering procession to a right angle. Note the aligned axial penetration of this distinct room, culminating in the fireplace. Note also the several outdoor rooms created by the formal crenellations.*

Figure 10 *Living room. Materials, colors, and axes interact to effect a quietly rich space.*

Figure 11 *Bedroom. The gable volume announced so distinctly on the exterior translates directly into a cathedralized room space. Note the use of paint as a delineator. Note also the corner window and the deck access (right).*

retical interpretations may be imposed over this house because it has the scale, variety, and above all integrity to support a multitude of ultimately unimportant analytic overviews.

Essentially this house uses axial circulation and a formal plinth of outdoor "street" to link together formally expressed interior rooms—rooms that are arranged in such a way as to form outdoor "rooms" between and around their expressed forms. In this way and others this house dramatically evidences some of the classic organizing concepts advocated by this book to effectively liberate any house from a sense of spatial constriction.

In a planning sense, the overtly axial entry promenade imposes an extended impact of the building's power upon the encounterer. The variation in room form and orientation on the first floor creates sequential surprise and evokes a curiosity that is only satisfied by exploration. The defined exterior rooms extend the perceived space of the various interior rooms. There is orientation of all the various rooms across 80 feet of uninterrupted alignment of door openings to a fireplace at the grand end and a minor window at the casual end. This makes the house seem even grander. The second floor creates the backbone circulation axis alluded to, and the use of decks extends the utility of the bedrooms.

All of these formal manipulations and planning orientations have environmental factors calculated into their formulation. The entire second floor has been analyzed to be self-venting during summer months. Shading devices are also integral. Structurally the short bay construction is quite easily effected.

The house makes quite an aesthetic mountain out of a variety of charming molehills. It is difficult to make a kinetic building poignant, or an elongated form graceful, or a linear composition full of delight—it is also difficult to make a 3100-square-foot home feel 1200 square feet larger than it is.

The interior finishes are finely detailed to enhance the variety encountered. Bedrooms have their ceilings cathedralized under the formally expressed gable roofs, also enhancing a sense of the lyric.

These two young architects represent the best hope for domestic architecture—highly educated professionals, sensitive to clients' needs, bold enough to reject past answers, and diligent enough to make their innovations effect maximum visceral payback and increased utility. Perhaps it is training or talent or luck, but whether a 400-square-foot cabin performs like a 1000-square-foot house or a 3000-square-foot house performs like a 4000-square-foot mansion, it is the architect who should receive the gratitude of his or her clients and the recognition of his or her constituency.

THE
SECOND
HOME

W hether a vacation home, retreat, studio, or secondary dwelling, the redundant domicile has many advantages of limits: limited occupancy, limited seasonal use, limited environmental focus, and often a very limited building budget. Second homes are the products of affluent abundance, but, paradoxically, they often evidence the very best astringent puritan values.

Often designed by architects as modern-day follies, or as semisculptural aesthetic distillations, or even as experiments in minimal human accommodation, these houses represent slightly stilted design responses to special situations of site, use, and budget.

Beyond these caveats of specialized utility, these homes are nonetheless homes. And while some may represent radical expressions of a personal aesthetic, none loses the common sense of human behavior.

As some sites evidence the heightened drama of waterside orientation and the programs evidence reduced functional versatility, perspective must be maintained. The aesthetic tools employed to create a maximal perception of space amid spatial constriction are applicable to any house. As with the full-use houses presented in the prior section, these homes are all the products of reduced space consumption, whether accommodating one or a dozen occupants.

In this way these examples, sequenced in ascending size, convey the essential message of this book: that no matter what site, budget, household need, or idiosyncratic aesthetics are applied to a house design, the virtues of a reduced building volume are manifold and conducive to innovation.

Rustic Romanticism

Arne Bystrom designs and builds a livable sculpture along the wild coast of Washington.

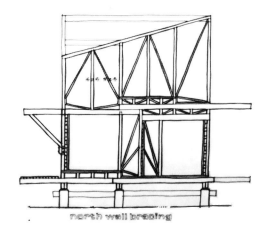

north wall bracing

No matter what their stylistic bias, architects often daydream of Piranesiesque visions of abstracted structure, heroic space, and powerfully impactive light. Whether the architect dreams of classical colonnades, organic vaults, or steel, string, wire, and glass catching light and defining space, the essential elements of all architectural delineation are manipulated in musings.

Arne Bystrom built his dream.

Over several years Bystrom and his family fabricated a 300-foot seaside retreat. What might have been a cabin, a shack, or even a civil vantage from which to view the raw beauty is instead the extraordinary implementation of one man's essential vision of architecture.

As the architect's statement articulates, the environmental obstacles implicit in building in a remote location were overcome by ingenuity and hard work. Similarly the seemingly eccentric construction is thoroughly designed to maximize structural efficiency as well as expressiveness.

Intimate knowledge keyed this poetic distillation of form and structure. Bystrom examined the needs of his family to the point where the spaces created were absolutely minimized, and thoroughly specialized to the point of functional exclusivity. Similarly Bystrom used a

---

ARCHITECT'S STATEMENT

The solution had three parts. First, minimum spaces were programmed for all family functions, namely cooking, eating, conversing, reading, and sleeping. These spaces were then rigidly designed to accommodate primarily one function. The spaces were isolated from each other by changes of level and screen walls. At the same time, the whole building volume was allowed to flow vertically and to a lesser extent horizontally so that this smallness would not be apparent.

Second, the framing of local cedar was expressed on the inside as the major architectural element. Stiffness was built into the very open structure by a pattern of horizontal bracing.

Third, the cabin was designed as a passive solar collector, which is so efficient that a fire is seldom needed. The clear Plexiglas roof catches heat even on gray days. The upper bunks are warm to awaken in even on cool winter mornings.

Arne Bystrom

LIST OF PARTICULARS

Bystrom cabin
Location: Coastal Washington
Architect: Arne Bystrom
Budget: Incalculable and irrelevant
Nominal space: 300 square feet
Perceived space: 500 square feet

---

structural system of diagonal struts, buttressing a post-and-beam construction and utilizing heavy cantilevers for decks. This system is the released energy of an architect intimately acquainted with the civilized use of heavy-timber construction.

There are distinct subspaces amid the cubic volume defined by this structural lattice. The living area is set at a lower level and focused on integral seating. Similarly, the dining area is focused on a sculptured dining table, and the kitchen is a simple space oriented to a counter and appliances. Sleeping is accommodated by two suspended double bunk beds nestled beneath the Plexiglas-glazed roof. Each of these subspaces has its expressed floor framing extended to create a deck or balcony. Amid all these thoroughly designed elements, Bystrom inserted stock sliding doors for in-fill glazing and deck access.

The site provided most of the building materials and determined the desire for a minimal intrusion by the building.

Unlike many other projects in this book, this house defies verbal description. Just as the imposition of money, engineering, and telephone calls can cause the pollution of an architectural fantasy, words would diffuse the poignance of this extraordinary work of art.

Figure 1 *Set on sonotube footings, a simple shed-roofed cubic volume is sheathed in 4-foot to weather cedar shingles and punctured by raw cantilevered decks, accessed by sliders. The lack of any railings evidences the extreme isolation of this structure.*

Figure 2 *Distant prospect. In a wind-swept, cliff-side posture, the tiny house form (middle left) fairly huddles beneath the trees.*

Figure 3 *Exposed skeleton. Diagonal bracing enlivens a simple post-and-heavy-timber construction. Note how the upper sleeping areas flank the corner living area and extend balconies out into the air beyond the envelope.*

Figure 4 *Open roof. Glazed with Plexiglas, this cross-framed roof diagonally connects the vertical structural elements. Bunk beds sit behind a freestanding tongue-and-groove partition looming above the living area below. Note the varieties of light levels present in this photo.*

3

4

5

6

7

Figure 5 *First floor. The dining area is in the foreground, the living area to the right, the entry to the left, the kitchen beyond the tongue-and-groove partition, and the bedroom lofts above. The extraordinarily casual quality of thoroughly handmade elements creates a rugged romanticism. Note the stump stools (left) and double ladder verticals at entry (left background). Note also the double-direction floor framing above and the descending light from the glazed roof.*

Figure 6 *Looking into living area. This photo shows three spaces, each oriented to a large glazed window, each feeding onto a deck, and each resting on a different level. The bedroom is to the upper left, the kitchen is behind the tongue-and-groove wall to the middle left, and the living area is everywhere else. Note the wire flue bracing between double-beam extension to the left, and the minideck extension from the bedroom to the upper left.*

Figure 7 *Entry. A secondary two-story space and entry are set above the dining area, which in turn is above the living area. Double ladders extend to the sleeping areas. Note the slot of roof view through the ladder. Note also the open prospect of outside brought inside (right).*

The Second Home   **115**

A True Tree House

Robert and Hedy Jacklin build an exquisite refuge set above the ground plane in rural Washington.

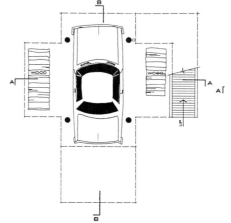

Extreme limits can be depressing. Housing a family of four in a 450-square-foot house—even a vacation house—is an extremely limiting design constraint.

If this book has a point, a one-liner synopsis, then it is that limits can liberate the creative mind. In a limitless world, where money, the laws of physics and nature, and the foibles of personal preference are thoroughly under control, the creative mind has no datum from which to apply itself. A fried egg has a perfect yolk amid the undulating albumen, a flapping flag has its flagpole, an effervescing symphony has its meter. Without definitive contexts, limits, and referential guidelines, life has no apprehendable measure. Music is played with musical instruments, and architecture accommodates individuals who spend a finite amount of money.

The Jacklins knew they wanted a retreat, an oasis in the forest, so they obtained a modest site close to a glacier-fed river and Mount Rainier. As with most young families, there was little or no money to spend on the frivolity of a second home, so this house would be owner-built.

All of the second-home or vacation-home projects in this book have several distinct advantages to their implementation as house designs. Obviously, reduced use, focused prospect, and limited spatial requirements impact favorably upon a building budget as a house can shrink and simplify. But this house displays a secondary benefit only do-it-yourselfers can truly appreciate. Only if you already have a place to live can you afford to spend 5 years building a home. And often unless you have 5 years to spend building, the limits of available hours and money can make a house such as this a fool's errand.

ARCHITECT'S STATEMENT

A pole building best solved the various problems of program and site. By having the first inhabited level of the building 9 feet above ground level, we would allow flood waters to pass beneath without causing damage.

The size of 450 square feet was arrived at as the smallest that would comfortably accommodate four people and still be buildable by ourselves within a reasonable period of time and at an affordable cost.

The open plan, with loft, maximizes the sense of space and views within this small building. My wife and I occupy the loft, and our two girls sleep below, on the built-in couch that opens out into a bed.

Total time of construction was 5 years.

Robert Jacklin

LIST OF PARTICULARS

Jacklin house

Location: Tacoma, Washington

Architect: Robert Jacklin

Budget: Tiny, and spent over 5 years, hence, somewhat meaningless

Nominal space: 450 square feet

Perceived space: 600 square feet

The Jacklin house is anything but foolish. Its extremely sophisticated use of minimum space for maximum impact is only fully appreciated when the plans and photos are closely compared. In the photos, there is a sense of a modest 1200-square-foot elevated cabin. The plans reveal that the level of considered design is such that this fully functional vacation house for four has been effected with less space than that of a typical living room of a standard raised ranch.

How was so much impact derived from so little material, space, and money? Architect-owner-builder Robert Jacklin used the fruits of rigorously reconsidering every aspect of human accommodation and designed the house to reflect the minimal spatial response divined as necessary. If the design process ended there, however, we might be left with a space capsule. Instead, the qualities of form and space have been addressed as well. Involved with these criteria is the intimate knowledge possessed by a man reconsidering his own family's needs.

The result is the spatial and formal product of three distinct elements:

1. *Pole-and-beam construction.* Inexpensive elevation and easy fabrication were achieved by using a system that required little excavation and few pieces and that allowed great versatility.

2. *A cruciform plan.* The square defined by four pole supports can have its sides extended (and its framing simply cantilevered) to effect enormous spatial variety with a minimum of support and literal delineation.

3. *A shed roof.* The most modest of roof

All photos by Robert Perron

Figure 1 *Back of the house. Cantilevers, poles, and air seem to support this assertive raked form. Note the alignment of the strip window to the entry cantilever at left and the visible stair ascending beyond the central window.*

Figure 2 *Deck end. Bypassing adjacent trees (right), the deck pushes out an additional 6 feet from the house mass. Note the embracing cantilever over the entry stairs (right) and the applied shelf on the tree trunk (center), evidencing an intimacy only Tarzan may appreciate fully. The wrapping of the deck and stair rails in shingles enhances a sense of a stretched exterior skin and ultimately allows for the final ascendancy of the proud prow of roof (upper right).*

Figure 3 *Living area, facing loft. Overtly vertical, this central focus of the house displays isolated elements of structure, stair, and stove, as well as subspaces of bedroom and kitchen. Note how the stair meshes with the wall system through the extension of its handrail over a lowered section of low wall—the wall being necessary to prevent unfortunate visual intrusion into the bedroom itself. Note the tree trunk beyond the bedroom window and the use of wood as ceiling material.*

Figure 4 *Living area. Facing northerly dining niche, the flanking seating–second-bedroom niche (left) and kitchen niche (right) sit amid the quiet forest of pole structure and heavy-timber bearing—all in close proximity to the central heat of a wood stove. Note the use of the seating underside for wood storage and the full-wall fixed glazing. Note also the gaps between all wood pieces and gypsum walls. Note last the loft cantilever (upper right) and the clerestory illumination above the dining area.*

Figure 5 *Underside. Normally, this area is occupied by a car; the drying logs that are shown here are close to being split. Diagonal steel cables provide lateral stability at ground level. Note that the stair-rail wall (right) harbors a light switch and an electric outlet and meter and that the water shutoff at the bottom of the stair is a proud fixture (well-used in seasonal occupancy).*

3

4   5

forms that actively sheds water, the shed roof requires only one plane of definition. It also has a powerful formal presence when applied with forethought.

*   *   *

This rudimentary list of the three essential components tells us just so much; a digression is in order to enrich the apprehension of this tiny home.

A 5 × 5 foot bay is implemented (with modest variations) throughout the plan of the house. The central square bay is four modules, while each wing of the cruciform cantilevers out by 5-foot extensions. Fine-tuning results in the stair width of 3 feet, 6 inches defining one wing and a cantilevered deck extending one wing to a full 10 × 10 foot, four-module bay. Each described wing has a tight-fitting function. A northern-sitting niche–cum–children's sleeping area stakes out one wing, a modest dining table another, a kitchen lending new meaning to the word "efficiency" takes up another wing, and the extended deck allows the last wing to serve as pure spatial release. A spiral stair connects the sleeping loft to the main-floor area. The loft itself is the last extension off the four-column array described. It cantilevers into the living-area central bay, and over the kitchen bay, and finally over the entry steps. The single bath is a double cantilever between the aforementioned loft wing and dining wing.

Power is conveyed formally by these massive cantilevers, which are facilitated by the tight column array and heavily cross-braced by the heavy-timber floor framing. Secondary benefits of this elevated posture are realized as well. Occasional floods and possible intruders are held at bay simply because the building is out of touch.

There are, of course, trade-offs in the realization of a minimalized building. There is no built-in storage, a wood stove provides the only heat, and access to the bath is through the loft bedroom space.

But these compromises are mitigated by the skillful application of the subsystems of walls, windows, and skin treatment and the utility of a thoroughly open underside of the house for storage. The single enclosing fabric utilized is cedar shingle for exterior walls and roof. Similarly, gypsum wallboard is used on all interior wall surfaces. In and of themselves, these materials are quite prosaic, but they are applied in consistent deference to the interior structural grid and exterior window locations. The interior beaming (up to 4 × 10 inch members) is allowed to run untouched by the enclosure walls, creating a marvelous sense of bypassing systems either enclosing space or passing through it. Secondarily the alignment and orientation of windows allow the shingle skin to have the uninterrupted planes that give it power.

The ascending raked roof rising finally above the bedroom-loft cantilever provides a proud head to the form, under which the free-standing stair can modestly provide access to the house.

All this activity is set above the ground plane by four 8-inch-diameter poles, cross-braced diagonally by steel cable at the ground level. These poles sit on 8-inch concrete pads. Just under the grade level, the poles are stabilized further by concrete collars cast about their perimeters.

Any building taking 5 years to construct has an enormous level of thought and care put into its fabrication and design. More intangibly, the lofted rakish form addressing the trees has the considered dynamism to thoroughly defeat the sense of a constricted house. Internally, the lofty vertical spaces created under the dramatic roofline relieve any sense of constriction within the close confines of the enclosing walls. In scale, form, and spreading ascendance, this house embraces its neighboring trees with a sympathetic sensibility.

Robert Jacklin has shown that the small house responds inordinately well to a nurturing design, fed on time, reinvention, and a willingness to accept limits as a means to an end. In this case the end is a thoroughly delightful monument to good design and familial love.

Barnyard Basilica

Stanley Tigerman and Margaret McCurry realize their agrarian-reform fantasies in a thoroughly inspired weekend home.

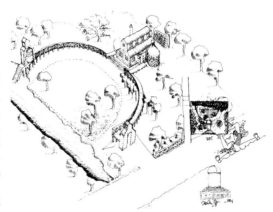

There may be no joy in Mudville, but there is ecstasy in Lakeside, Michigan. A rather ordinary site, a less than modest budget, and a prototypical second-home program have been massaged by Stanley Tigerman and Margaret McCurry into a lightly fantastic vehicle for their weekends away from Chicago.

Modest means have organized whimsy into a lusciously articulate shed-for-living. Tigerman and Mc Curry have taken pedestrian forms and materials and added a few Platonic ideals and a touch of true talent to effect an extraordinarily happy little home. Highly educated, worldly-wise folk, these two architects have meshed the stark charm of an extruded-basilica form and the innocence of applied latticework to compose a sophisticated ensemble, fraught with gentle humor and an uplifting spirit.

How is it that so many subtle sensibilities can be evoked within a 1000-square-foot building? Simply because the architects presented a clear hierarchy of parts upon which they layered the evocative elements which enrich their design. Without an essential form and organizational philosophy, the appliqués adorning any building become trite and shrill.

McCurry and Tigerman avoided the cheap thrill by investing time in the considered composition of the form created and the spaces defined. The layering of a successful design—especially a successful small-house design—begins with the abstracted consideration of how the basic pieces and parts interact. The skillful dialogues between the various identities effected literally set the stage for the charming elements applied to this house.

Virtually every element of successful small-house design considered in the introduction to this book is put into play

LIST OF PARTICULARS

Tigerman-McCurry house

Location: Lakeside, Michigan

Architects: Margaret McCurry and Stanley Tigerman

Budget: Not available

Nominal space: 1000 square feet

Perceived space: 1700 square feet

in this house. A series of axes and cross axes provides an enhanced perception of space. The central hall provides a marvelous vertical release upon entry and a spatial focus upon inhabitation. Standard elements of stock small-pane doors, galvanized-steel roofing, and chimney flue are used in fresh ways. Custom elements—ladder stair, ornamental lattice, and built-in sofa frame—are used as crucial focal points within the context of the main space. A simply symmetrical form facilitates a thoroughly ordinary framing plan. Color creates enhanced identities. Scale is varied between the tiny (the gable window) and the grand (the central hall). Avuncular "window dressing" (the exterior latticework and detached corncrib–screened porch) extends the exterior impact of the house. In short, the architects found ample opportunity in 1000 square feet of space to create engrossing interplay and delightful objectification.

The following grossly simplified description is offered to elucidate a short-form tour guide to the house. A two-part harmony of barn and corncrib (or basilica and baptistery) presents itself to the encounterer. The barn-basilica has four implicit bays, indicated by locally centered windows. The corncrib-baptistery is oriented to one bay on the exterior, while the interior of the house uses the two central bays to define the limits of a large-scale two-story central living space. The two flanking bays are subdivided both vertically and horizontally. Two lofts are neatly inserted into the reduced roof gable and are used for children's sleeping accommodations, while the wider first floor divides the bays into two couplets—kitchen-bath at one end (marrying wet functions) and master bedroom—

1

All photos by Howard N. Kaplan

2

Figure 1 *Entry. Basilica-baptistery, barn-corncrib, house-screened porch: the two-part harmony is both historically allusive and endearingly bucolic. Note how the prosaic materials blend with the classic dialogue between the linear and the centered.*

Figure 2 *Back of the house. Back doors and fireplace provide focus and scale to a semi-industrial building. Note how the circular patio to the right forms a shadow of the screened porch present on the entry side of the house.*

3

4

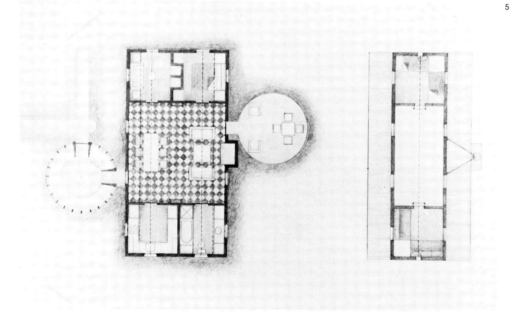

5

Drawings by the architects

Figure 3 *Gable end. Proudly laminated with a fine lattice, the flattened facade is punctured by three diminutive windows, emphasizing the quality of an applied fabric.*

Figure 4 *Night view. Solid rotunda becomes lattice-trapped space capped with a standing seam sheet-metal bonnet. Note how the central double doors shine through the applied filigree.*

Figure 5 *Plans. First floor (left) is a simple 20 × 40 foot rectangle subdivided into four bays: the end bays (serving wet functions) bottom, the master bedroom and the den to the top, and the central double bay with a double-height spatial focus. The long axis links the front (left) to the back (right) facades. Note the absence of the ultimately constructed entry air lock adjacent to the semidetached rotunda. Note also the mirrored shadow of the footprint of the circular screened porch. The upper level (right) presents two square lofts, axially oriented but separated, over the void of the living area.*

6

Figure 6 *Stair. Custom ladder stair reinvents vertical access, as outsized bull-nosed treads (echoed by low wall edge above) form a sculptured ascendance to a symbolic threshold. Note the handrails. Note also the door-centered lighting, the pull-down shade on the glass bedroom door, and the beckoning loft space, all providing delightful detail and spatial variety to the composed interior.*

Figure 7 *Fireplace facade. Lattice-backed seating, ornamented fireplace, small-pane glazed doors, and clerestory windows all reinforce an ordering central axis. Note the ascending space trapped by the loft to the upper left.*

Figure 8 *Interior axis. The basilica form creates an open interior with subdivided ends. Facing the master bedroom below—and the sleeping loft–cum–choir loft above—a centered interior facade proudly fills the vertical void. Custom ladder, stair, and flanking small-pane doors combine with the central threshold to create a large-scale facade in a small-scale house. Note how the right door aligns with the window to effect a long-range linkage. Note the clerestory window (upper left) and the ceiling fan hanging from the dropped roof to the peak beam. Flanking intermediate beams are obscured by the corners of the dropped ceiling. These beams prevent the need for tierods or collar-tie beams. Note the landscaped seating in the foreground, defining a central subspace.*

7

study at the other (isolating private functions). These opposing end bays have linking axial orientations aligning windows, doors, sink, toilet, and furniture to effect large-scale order in a small-scale context.

Space flows across the grand area, is trapped by cells below, and ascends to open lofts above. Amid all the spatial play, opposing custom ladder stairs and loft entry portals provide positive elements, while a lattice-wall-linked sofa ensemble stakes out the central focus of the grand hall.

The axial house form with its extruded shape and beveling roof is perfectly counterpointed by the screened pavilion-cum-rotunda. Radial symmetry has a civilized discourse with bilateral symmetry. The Renaissance lives in Michigan. But so do farms, and the barnyard allusions of the formal interplay are no less legitimate.

Amid all the educated posturing sit recognizable stock components of corrugated-steel siding and roofing, chrome-plated chimney flue, and poignant rafter vents. Internally, esoteric light fixtures stand in concert with standard drafting lamps and ceiling fans.

There is no basement and little storage area or sleeping area amid all these idealized interactions, but the kitchen and bath are luxurious by 1000-square-foot house standards.

Extreme care is evidenced by all these deliberate ordinations and juxtapositions. Lyric allusion becomes rambling babble without a thoughtful consideration of context and priorities.

This wondrously sophisticated home maintains its humility and hence its meaning. It may be said that this domestic tranquility is due to the artful insight of its designers, and that is true, but it is also definitely attributable to an astringent budget affording a financial datum that no sensible designer would attempt to deny. Down-to-earth does not necessarily mean down-and-dirty, and the bucolic poignance of the farm has a dignity this house successfully aspires to.

Created to house the Tigermans' two most precious collaborative efforts (children) as well as evidence an aesthetic artistry, this home presents the contrasting truths of utility and grand design. The simple harmonies effected are both timeless and charged with the creative spark.

8

Ascendance

Roger Ferri creates a classically kinetic beach house.

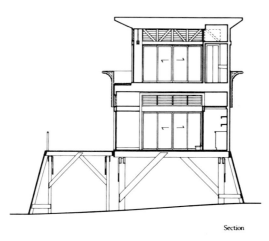

Section

Elegance is elusive. Applying ornament to effect stature and grace is a hollow cosmetic gesture. Expanding size to aggrandize a building's scale merely postures bloat for impact. Creating a distorted aesthetic distillation merely denies a human utility in favor of a scaleless sculpture-for-living. Abiding elegance is born of an integral combination of formal distinction, functional accommodation, and innovatively articulate detailing.

Words are cheap, and the description of vague criteria for excellence is pale in contrast to the depth of delight found in an elegant building.

Architects designing vacation homes can accept the challenges of limited occupancy and extreme environmental orientation and use these focusing criteria to create buildings of extraordinary impact, or they can ignore the potentials presented. Architects betray the promise of their profession if they create houses in strident competition with their sites or if they sit on their aesthetic hands and create expressionless human accommodation in deference to powerful sites.

Roger Ferri took up the challenge of a minimalist program and an exquisite site and created a building of unique presence and power. The program was indeed simple: a house was to be designed to accommodate two to six people, with only one fixed bed location. The site was indeed spectacular: Water Island, New York, a sandbar-cum-island on the Atlantic Ocean off Long Island is essentially an uninterrupted stretch of sand and water.

Ferri recognized that added height could be used to afford spatial distinction and formal expression to the direct and uninterrupted view. A tripartite layering was effected: A code-compliant first-floor

---

ARCHITECT'S STATEMENT

A beach house is the setting for a care-free mind and a soaring spirit. This is conveyed through form in the lyricism of composition. To create visual lightness the volumes become increasingly transparent, smaller in size, and more chromatic as they get higher. Uplifting lines of sunscreens and overhangs levitate toward weightlessness.

Roger Ferri

LIST OF PARTICULARS

Blum house

Location: Water Island, New York

Architect: Roger Ferri

Budget: Not available

Nominal space: 1200 square feet

Perceived space: 1600 square feet

---

elevation was attained by utilizing an uncompromising plinth upon which sits an architectural couplet of timeless impact. The actual house pulls its perimeter back from the plinth edge and centers its form on the defined plane. The crowning second story further retracts its mass concentrically from the first-floor perimeter. Stepped massing is not implicitly graceful, but the grace of this beach house is undeniable.

The essential formal tool employed by Ferri to give his composition both distinction and power is the use of extended pavilion eaves, which effect a weightless linearity.

Undersides are often hidden in architecture; the plinth of this project uses lattice to obscure its underside and to create a sense of monolithic mass supporting the stepped pavilions. But in this particular project, the horizontal spread of the formal slabs is counterpointed by the spreading extension of, first, deck edge, then, roof eave. An aerodynamic sensibility is imposed; the cantilevered eaves serve as formal air foils to loft the first step of massing. Eaves are often aesthetically gratuitous devices oriented to create shade, direct wind, or shed water, but these overhangs, while performing all the functions listed above, also celebrate their own construction; the careful joinery and quality materials engender a sense of considered detail.

The planning of this small home was relentlessly reductionist. The entire house was kept to 1200 square feet. All serving spaces of bath, stair, closet, kitchen, and utility access were linearly condensed into a 4-foot-deep wall set to the landward side of the plan. This density allows for thorough spatial release, creating two stacked open plan spaces, each unencumbered on three sides.

All photos by Cervin Robinson

Figure 1 *South. As the form steps back from defined perimeters, eaves launch and glass and paint begin to dominate the house exterior. Note the chamfered plinth edge and the lattice-shrouded shower sitting on it.*

Figure 2 *Eaves. Note the lattice-shrouded plinth, public middle, and private top. Natural materials tightly detailed into dynamic forms evidence both craftsmanship and careful design. The architect uses shadow in close concert with form and material to effect an enormous aesthetic depth. Tuscan columns are applied as ornament to the pavilion corners. Note that the middle lattice lip is formed on curved verticals supporting built-in seating. Note also the louvered glazing below the triumphantly levitated final eave.*

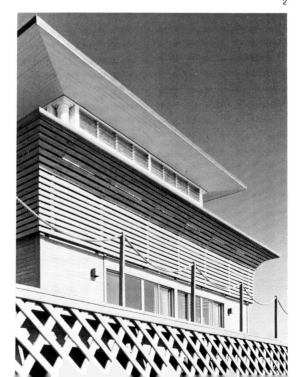

3

Figures 3 and 4 *Section. The solidity of the plinth is shown to be an erroneous assumption as the house structure remains independent from it. The curving lattice lip is revealed to be a simple application, banded about the entire building. Note the transom louver glazing above the sliding glass doors and the deep-wall service zone oriented to the single aligned wall plane.*

Figure 5 *Living space. Storage, stair, and wet areas are found in the deep wall to the right. The lowered height of these condensed spaces mitigates their imposition on the open area. Note the extra sleeping accommodations. Note also the interior plywood surface treatment, with aligned seaming and uninterrupted even spacing, and the continuous moulding lines oriented to the sliding-window height and curtain rod. The simple extension of the floor plane into the deck plinth expands the perceived space. The detailing throughout this essential enclosure of space is both thoroughly ordered and passive.*

Figure 6 *Bedroom. A glazed pavilion opens to the sea. Note the blank wall (right), obscuring the dense-packed service spaces. Here, as in the living area, slider heights are defined with light moulding treatments as they wrap around the space, ultimately extending to form the lowered track for a room-dividing screen. The exposed trusses collect the substantial loads of the long-span framing and cantilevered roof above and define a transom space where glass louvers admit diffused lighting and emit stale or overheated air.*

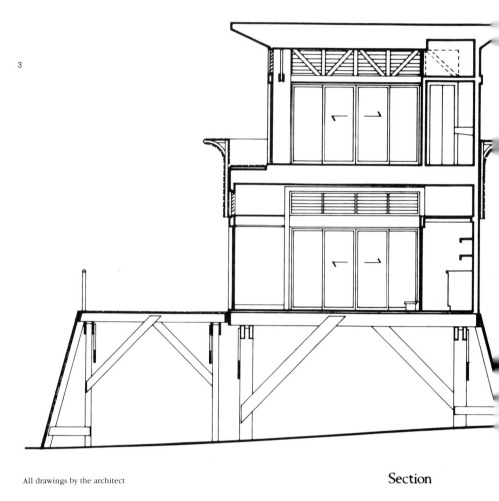

All drawings by the architect

Section

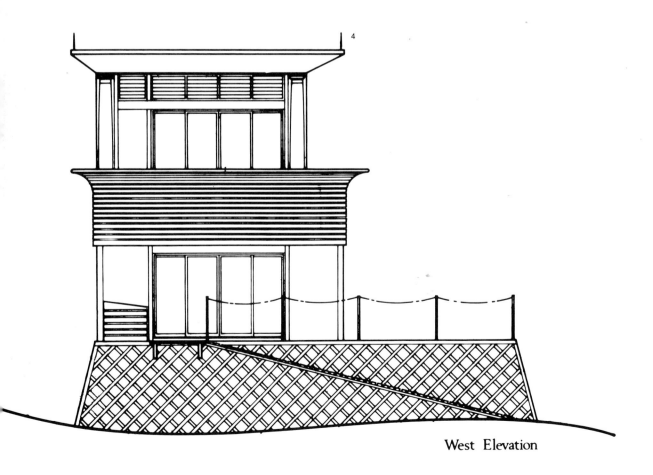

4

West Elevation

5

6

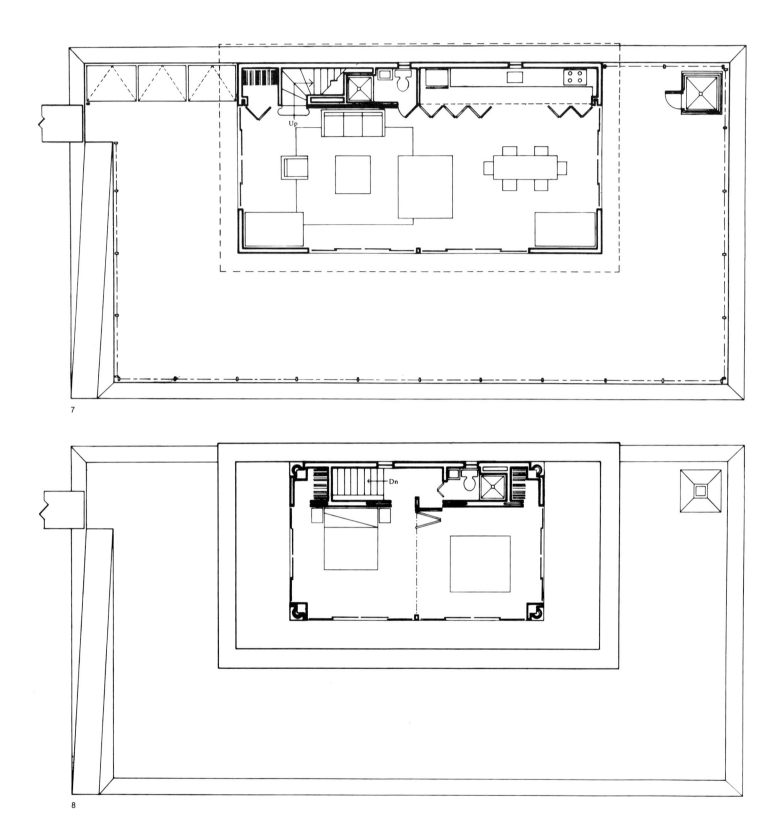

7

8

Figure 7 *First floor. Set amid the placid plane of an extended deck plinth, this simple rectangle (close to being a double square in plan) has all its service functions coalesced into a single deep wall along the non-view-oriented side. This dense bay extends left to define the storage bins and right to locate a freestanding shower. Note that the entry bridge (left) aligns with the room-side edge of this bay. Note also the water-accessing ramp integrated with the plinth edge to the left. The three rectangles (in the corners and at the center) are secondary sleeping accommodations.*

Figure 8 *Sleeping loft. An open space with three strip-glazed walls, this room shows that the service-space deep wall effected on the first floor extends to this level as well. Note the extensive use of pocket doors and the collapsible partition. Note also the wraparound deck and ornamental corner columns.*

The plinth provides ample spatial overflow, and the living, dining, and cooking areas (plus a full bath for guest use) are confined to the first floor. The second floor is given over to another bath and a single sleeping space, subdividable into two bedrooms via an integral folding partition. Wrapping about this bedroom pavilion is the secondary benefit to the stepping formal expression, a wraparound deck. The spreading deck rail edge—effected simply through the use of distinct slats attached to curved ribs—serves as a seating area and a screening device to prevent visual intrusion from those plinth dwellers who might otherwise catch a peek looking up into the open bedroom. Because this rail is low, bed inhabitants have an uninterrupted view of the water.

The open plans described have structural consequences. Given the large-scale openings, which provide an unframed visual link with the water, given the lack of columns or partitions to pick up the significant loads generated, and given especially the discontinuity of bearing walls due to the formal stepping, large headers had to be employed to span over the glazed voids in the walls. The headers needed depth to provide adequate support. Rather than simply bury a discreet steel I beam or wooden box beam above the glazing, Ferri both expressed and utilized the structure he had imposed on the project. First of all, ceiling heights were raised to accommodate the structural members above the standard 6-foot, 8-inch door height. Second, an open-web truss was imposed for support above the window walls. Last, these clerestory or transom-height wall spaces were glazed with operable louvers, providing ambient light when drapes are drawn to prevent overheating and to allow venting of stale air without the enormous sea breeze drafts a seaside location can cause. By meshing structure, fenestration, and environmental regulation, Ferri met the challenge of designing in functional utility along with the intangibles of aesthetics.

In a similar manner, Ferri combined materials to enhance their impact and create the sense of scale small houses can seldom aspire to. As said, the lattice-wrapped plinth has its form effectively defined by chamfered sides and mute corner detailing. Note that a simple rope rail further enhances the seemingly monolithic stasis of the plinth form.

The second tier (the living pavilion) has the edge of its lower band defined by the top edge of the sliding glass door array. Above the glazing, the horizontal banding is made three-dimensional by use of horizontal latticework, held off the facade and finally curving outward to effect the expressed edge. It should be noted that the leading edge of this deck raid–cornice–visual screen–seat has been bull-nosed and painted red—a striking datum from which the sleeping temple emerges.

The third tier (save the backside) is simply a glazed rectangle with ornamental Tuscan columns at the corners. This last, capping pavilion has its nonglazed parts painted white. Especially effective is the painted eave underside, gently canted and covered with tongue-and-groove material.

Each layer has a top, middle, and bottom, echoing the entire built form and alluding to classical principles that are universally appealing.

In capturing the potential of the site, Roger Ferri served his clients well. In expressing the forms he divined with both power and sophistication—implementing contrasting materials, strong shadow lines, and subtle engineering—Ferri gave his clients an unforgettable house.

With allusions to Egyptian or Minoan Revival architecture, or echoes of ziggurat massing or gentle Classicist organization, this building is simply and poetically elegant.

Aspiring Domicile

Mark Simon creates a focused fantasy on Long Island for his musical mother.

When designing buildings, architects often resort to invoking the abstract world of systems, orders, and methodologies. Such linearization of creativity provides an overlay of conscientious planning on a potentially chaotic process. These efforts at regulating complex mental machinations can serve to generate design criteria, or they can simply rationalize retroactively a serendipitous fait accompli.

Standing in joyous contrast to Cartesian justification is the Crowell house by Mark Simon. If serendipity is manifest in this book, it is in the form of this tiny house located on the shore of Long Island. In the best spirit of creative irrationality, this delightful confection evokes a genuine sense of unconditional positive regard toward those in its presence.

Powerfully beckoning via its overtly vertical orientation, this music studio–cum–second home also points the way to the sea. The architect has made the home formally evocative, but more than that, he has provided it with the means for immediate processional seduction. A meandering exterior ascent is covered by a simple extension of the roof plane, which becomes a tiny entry portico at ground level. No less than five sets of level changes, located to encourage oblique encounter, ultimately lead the occupant through the house to the final reward of a tower-top view.

The unapologetic whimsy of this home embodies the very lyric spirit it was meant to house. Designed primarily as a refuge for musical composition with a secondary intention toward habitation, this home presents a unique form created from familiar parts.

The delightful ascension into and up through the house is the dominant expe-

ARCHITECT'S STATEMENT

This small house is a composer's studio on the shore in the Hampton dunes of Long Island. Large enough to serve as a vacation house for rental or future sale, it adjoins a permanent residence next door.

Reminiscent of Long Island windmills and lighthouses, an octagonal tower domed with lead-coated copper is the building's core. Hip roofs slope off the tower to the north, protecting it from winter winds. Large double-hung windows face south to gain the sun's warmth. Roofs and walls are of red cedar shingles, and cedar latticework abounds in rails and porch overhangs.

The success of this house, we think, lies in its rambling seaside spirit. Designed with a romantic gesture, it reminds some of an old man looking out to sea, his capes flowing behind him. While it fondly remembers old and fast-disappearing Long Island neighbors, it makes no pretense of belonging to any but our own time.

Mark Simon

LIST OF PARTICULARS

Crowell house

Location: Long Island, New York

Architect: Mark Simon, assisted by Leonard J. Wyeth III

Budget: Not available

Nominal space: 1300 square feet

Perceived space: 1300 square feet

riential theme. The external focus of all the pedestrian ascendancy is the exquisite water view. The formal hierarchy of the building is in thorough service to the crowning glory of the project, its leaden dome. Stair, view, and dome combine to create procession, context, and goal—a sequence that has seldom been so poignantly distilled.

It is in the innocent posturing of the house that allusive interpretations may run rampant. But in truth this is no picture-postcard fantasy; Mark Simon has simply had the opportunity and creative insight to form a house based on experiential values rather than abstract ideology. Unpainted shingles left to weather; octagonal towers; double-hung windows; latticework; standing seam, lead-shrouded, cupola-crowned domes; and white-painted trim are all traditional architectural elements. However, when set in the rigorously prioritized procession by Simon, they are merely means to an end.

The limited programmatic requirements helped in the effort to prioritize. Bath, kitchen, and bedroom could be extraordinarily diminutive. However, fully one-third of the constructed house was given to the rambling ascent to the tower top. The remaining studio, dining, and loft spaces were each made special by their backwater character, bypassed by the grand march. A paucity of readily accessible storage space is also understandable given the highly specialized use. The house sits at a code-required elevated level, which facilitates a garage and storage space slightly below grade.

Perhaps the underlying theme of this work is its recognition of picturesque organization as a legitimate design criterion. Animated elements such as a false chimney, lattice banding, and winding

Lizzie Himmel

Figure 1 *West, entry. An extension of greeting, this architectural pseudopod in the form of miniportico merely brings the grand scale of a distant dome down to earth. Wrapping bands of lattice and painted moulding enhance the animation and order the whimsy. Note that the chimney is merely a shingle-shrouded plumbing vent stack and heating plant flue, with an ornamental cap. In this way the twentieth century is obscured in favor of something more ambiguous.*

Figure 2 *South, procession. The banding either flows away from or reaches out to the dominant octagonal form. The magic of enclosed but exterior subspaces helps invite occupancy. Note the spatial pinch at the entrance (left) and the ascending roofline, releasing the entrant to the sea prospect— all under the protective wing of the house itself.*

Figure 3 *North, back of the house. Affording no view, no solar gain, and no desire for visual intrusion from the outside world, this is truly the service entrance. The slightly sunken carport (center) leads to a storage area below. Note the glint of light piercing through the elevated underside of the house.*

Centerbrook Architects

Centerbrook Architects

2

3

Himmel

4

5   Lizzie Himmel

Centerbrook Architects   6

Figure 4 *The dome. Shrouded in lead-coated copper, this romantic element is detailed to withstand the ages. A marvelous combination of fine craftsmanship, ingratiating depth, and giddy ascendance, this compositional focal point is loaded with personal appeal.*

Figure 5 *The promised promontory. The citadel, the minaret, the crow's nest, or the cockpit, this tiny space captures a breathtaking view and provides the isolated context for musical invention. Note the stair cover in the foreground, and note that this shot was taken from outside the space through a window opposing the door.*

Figure 6 *Recessional procession. Looking back to the point of entry, this view shows how several level changes, a winding path, ever-increasing roof height, and porch opening create a sense of conspired progression.*

Figure 7 *Entrance. Lurking behind the potted shrub, the front door dominates one of the beveling facets of the house facade along the path of the exterior stair seen from the inside. The transition to the next level—the half-level ascendance to the bedroom (through the door) and to the point of departure for the final aspiring act—seduces the entrant up the stairway to the promised dome. It is good to note that only two geometries (an orthogonal wall layout and a 45° chamfering wall system) are employed to create this ongoing flow. Note the ascending window heights (right) and ceiling height (above) and the functional hub for the entire house, the piano. Note also the thick, sound-absorptive rug. Note last the octagonal arch over the half-level change, repeating the plan motif.*

Figure 8 *Floor plan. Entry is fronted by a portico (left) and is progressively released both in terms of passage width and ceiling height. As half levels ascend and wind into the house, the studio (note dashed skylights), the dining room, and the bedroom are left in the processional wake. Note the tiny unit kitchen and intimate bath. All the displayed energy is made possible by the considered imposition of 45° beveling, culminating in the octagonal tower plan.*

Lizzie Himmel

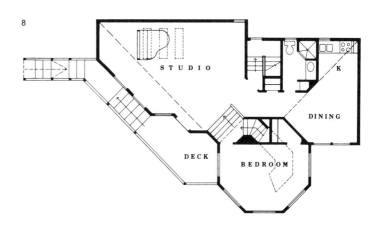

STUDIO

K

DINING

DECK

BEDROOM

Drawing by the architect

stairs have a personally ingenuous quality that cannot be thoroughly rationalized. All the elements of the house are positioned, organized, and detailed to win over our spirits to an aspiring elevation.

But to say that this is a stage-set folly is absurd given the level of formal, spatial, and detailing sophistication evidenced. Mark Simon has brought the tools of an experienced architect to bear upon the extremely sensitive task of experientially derived, personally scaled house design. Given that the client was his mother, the level of focus and insight was heightened and personalized.

This is neither a product of a vision of the future nor a remembrance of the past. It is a product of the living ascendant spirit in all people. It is one of the few buildings that evidence overt optimism without synthetic artifice. Would that all homes had its spark of life.

Double Distraction

A deck and roof are used by Fox and Fowle to create extended utility and formal impact.

A three-bedroom summer residence contained in 1700 enclosed square feet does not leave much room for architectural expression—unless you can see that simple gestures can be made dramatic by uncompromising implementation. In short, the familiar can become bold in the presence of a clear-thinking architect.

The beginning of the design process for a vacation house is the addressing of the situation. In this case a narrow lot opens up to a beautiful lagoon on Martha's Vineyard as the topography rapidly descends to the water.

Essentially the site was quite harmonious with the program of a house capable of sleeping five in three bedrooms. The budget allowed for far fewer than 2000 square feet to be built, but with the reduced usage a waterside home can allow, there was adequate space, if the architects were creative enough.

Fox and Fowle Architects is a firm that meticulously describes its projects in working drawings. The architects thoroughly inspect the latent potential in simply constructed building forms. In this particular case, the properties of the existing site were exploited for the maximal visual linkage to the lovely lagoon view. Obviously there is nothing singularly inspirational about capturing a view, but here there is an exploitation of two aspects of the house that transforms both its image and its utility to a level of impact far beyond the enclosed 1700 square feet.

Violating a simple form in building a house can focus inordinate monies to effect convoluted results. However, extensions of normally described surfaces can stretch the perception of the house and expand its available space without

ARCHITECTS' STATEMENT

The Klein house, a small vacation house, is perched atop spectacular 30-foot-high bluffs and overlooks a picturesque lagoon in Oak Bluffs, Martha's Vineyard. The house is surrounded on two sides by neighboring houses, and we designed it to take advantage of the sloping site and to provide necessary privacy and seclusion. The L-shaped plan of the upper level winds around an outdoor deck facing all views, while the lower level, partially below grade, houses the bedrooms and utility areas. Because the traditional rooflines are carried to grade at the entrance elevation, the Klein house achieves a unique contemporary character in scale with the dramatic sandy bluffs below, while at the same time it harmonizes with its neighbors.

Fox and Fowle Architects

LIST OF PARTICULARS

Klein house

Location: Martha's Vineyard, Massachusetts

Architects: Fox and Fowle Architects

Budget: Not available

Nominal space: 1700 square feet

Perceived space: 2000 square feet

necessarily bloating the volume of enclosed space or breaking the bank. In the Klein house designed by Fox and Fowle, a roof is extended to reach its eave down to the ground cover, while a floor is extended to become a deck and nearly double the usable area in fair weather. The rudimentary elements of this house are the starting points to these extensions, and a simple description of the evidenced formal evolution is in order.

Essentially, a simple rectangular foundation is incised into the steeply sloping ground plane described, effecting an open end to the water and a buried end to the street. Above this basement a single-hip roof is directly projected up from one corner of the foundation and given an asymmetrical return to the water view, allowing for an open facade addressing the lagoon. The floor built above the foundation is simply extended in the direction opposite the low-roof side of the house, creating an expansive deck also addressing the water. On top of this deck is added a screened porch, held distinct from the rectangular house in plan but embraced by the simple extension of the roof plane to create a secondary wing. Between the expressed porch and the house is the entry to the whole ensemble.

Without the boldly lowered eave height and extended deck—extended beyond the normal, expectable limits, enough to accommodate a screened porch—this house would not be particularly extraordinary. But simple insights well expressed can make all the difference.

The three bedrooms and two baths take up more square footage than the kitchen and the modest living area (its

KLEIN RESIDENCE
Site Plan

Figure 1 *Site plan. A simple sliver addressing the water, the site provides perfect over-water sunsets and an adequate grade change for an inexpensive deck (cross-hatched) and private, view-oriented bedrooms below the entry level. Note how the car access is held thoroughly distinct from the house itself.*

Figure 2 *Entry. The entry is nestled between the dominant roof and the obscured screened porch (left). The roof reaches up and over the entry as the deck wraps about; the two elements are linked as the deck edge becomes the eave line. Violations of the entry (note the water vista visible through the building) and the roof-hip skylight (note the prefabricated venting unit set into the custom glazing) create foci amid the interfacing planes. Note the hidden gutters set behind the massive eave boards.*

All drawings by the architects

All photos by Dan Cornish

3

4

Figure 3 *Water end. Here, the deck is dominant. With bedrooms set at grade below living areas above (left), the deck is built over an intermediate ground level. Note that the rail is created by custom seating. Note also that the deck gives way to the house's gable end, with its termination keyed to the sliding glass door (center) and the secondary bedroom glazing below. Simple forms expressed directly in civilized discourse can effect a controlled dynamic of line and form.*

Figure 4 *South. The deck becomes a walkway as the applied screened porch (right) constricts the available deck space. The pinch creates the anticipation of the wonderful view—an anticipation well rewarded. Note the perfect shade vehicle of a lofty conifer, and the synthetic equivalent—applied bris soliel—which wraps about the entire south and west walls at door-header level.*

reduced size effected because of the deck extension). So the basement houses the sleeping accommodations, opening up to the water, while the uninhabitable area under the dropped eave on the floor above can be given over to dead storage space without sacrifice. The extended deck provides entry space, a plinth for the porch, and a marvelous low-cost vantage to take in the water.

There is, of course, clever detailing to bring light into the back of the hipped-roof space (a custom corner skylight), to objectify the roofscape (hidden gutters), and to provide a civilized, open barrier at the deck edge (integral custom seating).

Axes are reinforced between screened porch and house and between stair bottom and basement egress. The plan layout condenses storage area and provides wonderful views for all the inhabited spaces.

In short this is a simultaneously inspired and polished design solution. Both drama and utility are enhanced while costs are kept low. A maximum "bang for the buck" results, giving the clients a gift of well-done design work that will only gain luster as the house is used.

It is indeed a pleasure to see innovation transform such a simple house into a unique image, without costly reinventions and with enhancement of the integration to the site. Such is the nature of thorough work done with a lively eye.

Figure 5 *Fireplace. The only internally focused space, the elevated hearth provides an interior reward for the occupant. Note the 4 × 8 inch roof framing and the tie beam to the right. Note also the door to the right accessing the storage area defined under the low roof form shown in the exterior photos. Last, note the "heatilator" gratings, helping to obtain some net heat gain from the fire.*

Figure 6 *Basement. Three bedrooms and two baths are efficiently laid out to fill in the defined simple rectangular foundation. Note that only the bottom and right legs retain earth, while the three bedrooms open out to grade level. The master bedroom (upper left) has a double exposure, while the bedroom to the upper right has no water view. Note the circulation axis down the center of the plan, and the dashed deck perimeter with interior pier supports.*

Figure 7 *Entry floor. Essentially, this floor has three parts: the rectilinear house, enclosing under-roof storage (top and right), kitchen, dining room, half bath, and living room; the deck (bottom, cross-hatched), accommodating entry at right, view at left; and the screened porch (center bottom), partially enclosed but opening up to view. Note that the dashed lines above the south and west walls indicate sun-screening bris soliel.*

5

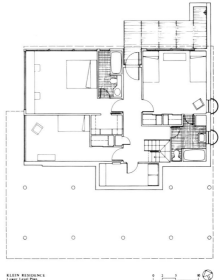

6

KLEIN RESIDENCE
Lower Level Plan
0 2 5 10

7

KLEIN RESIDENCE
Upper Level Plan
0 2 5 10

Polygonal Perch

Alfred DeVido manipulates plywood, dimensional lumber, and space into a crystalline revelation of singular impact.

Architecture is a dialogue of various elements, built, used, and experienced. In the mixture of structure, form, space, light, texture, and sensual manipulation, architects more often than not neglect certain parts in favor of others. Whether by subliminal prejudice or premeditated bias, small houses can suffer from an aesthetic reductio ad absurdum, not unlike the way the considered enjoyment of a good food can be preempted by an overwhelming spice.

In this context of potential distortion, Alfred DeVido, a New York architect, was asked to design a vacation house in Delaware.

Given a very tight site and a design program that required four bedrooms and large social areas, DeVido was faced with a stiff challenge. As with most new buildings built on coastal sites, this house had to respect both stringent federal restrictions regarding structural design and physical limitations of the building's organization.

The temptation in dealing with so much design input is to fix a singular perspective on the design of the building. Architects couch such arbitrary distillations of intent and form in metaphors, such as the house being a "wall" or a "cube" or a "screen." Fortunately, Al DeVido knows that a house is a building and that as such it has to have a mix of parts that has not only purpose but also enhancing diversity.

It is in the magic interplay of expressed structure, animated geometry, and consistent formal manipulation that DeVido enables a small house to have both power and depth.

Simply described, an interior wall sys-

ARCHITECT'S STATEMENT

The house was designed to serve as a weekend and vacation retreat for a Washington, D.C., family (six people, in all). It is located in Bethany Beach, Delaware, a seaside resort with high-density zoning. Since neighboring houses blocked the direct ocean view, we oriented the major spaces to catch an oblique glimpse of dunes and sea.

Because of the nearness of the ocean, federal flood-insurance rules required the house be set on piles, with the lowest living floor above mean high sea level. To avoid the awkward look of a house on stilts, we surrounded the lower-level pilings with textured cedar plywood. This was acceptable under the regulations governing "knock out" construction, and the room serves well as overflow space on busy weekends.

Alfred DeVido

LIST OF PARTICULARS

Wertheimer house

Location: Bethany Beach, Delaware

Architect: Alfred DeVido

Budget: $148,000

Nominal space: 2000 square feet

Perceived space: 2550 square feet

tem of bleached cedar plywood, a structure of bared dimensional lumber, and a geometry of 45° facets beveling the rectilinear system of walls are mixed in counterpoint to create a small home of powerful impact and yet subtle intentions. An orthogonal column grid has its corners chamfered and its form mitered until the original order becomes incidental to the perceived progression of building parts. Planes of plywood, webs of lumber, and pools of space are both ordered by cogent organization and animated by human encounter. Systems of fenestration, lighting, furnishings, and mill work actively respond to and reinforce the definitive progression of geometric articulation.

The water view, diagonal to the lot lines, is focused upon by the major space defined by the interacting grids. Certain plan elements of deck, stair, and master bedroom are formally and spatially assertive, while subdominant bedrooms, baths, and ancillary spaces simply coalesce into the posture of supportive infill.

Vertically the unoccupiable plinth of garage, entry, and storage, shrouded in black-stained plywood, supports the broad, double-height midsection, which in turn is crowned by the pyramidal master bedroom. A formal progression from recessive to animated to dominant is thus effected.

Amidst the potentially stultifying bilateral symmetry, a major axis is created by the juxaposition of two gable forms. Physical entry and spatial release are thus coordinated as a dynamic formal and sequential duet. The second dialogue, between northerly agglomerated bed-

1

Figure 1 *North entry. The middle girdle of clapboards fairly floats above a black-stained plywood skirt. Entry is keyed to the gable (right) and its somewhat symbolic trellis, which is wrapped around a custom fixed window. Placid above the beveling planes of the second floor, the master bedroom, crowned by a pyramidal roof and roof vent, proudly asserts its centered omnipotence. Note the final, punctuating wood-stove flue.*

Figure 2 *Plans. The first floor is a necessary podium for access, storage, and the apprehension of a distant view. It also accommodates stringent federal regulations for construction near water. On the second floor, a northerly density of spaces defines a multifunctional living room to the south. Stair and deck–screened porch serve as subdominant spots-in-the-plan. The third floor simply houses a bedroom and provides access to the fourth floor, the location of the master bedroom suite—a perfectly secure terminus to a great deal of architectural articulation.*

Figure 3 *Night view, south. Layers of space, light, and structure reveal themselves through the major axis vista presented. Note the deck in the forefront, followed by the screened porch, living area, wood stove, and balcony.*

3

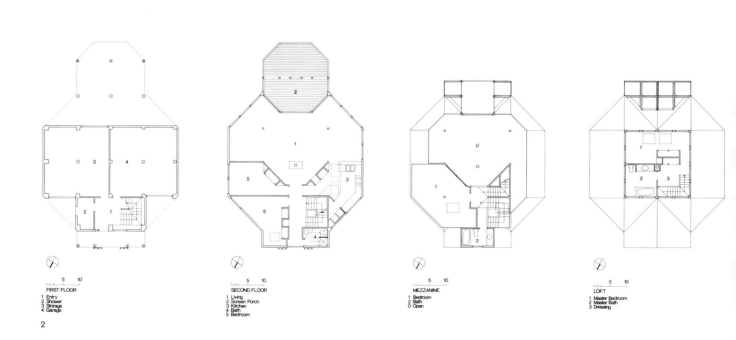

FIRST FLOOR

1 Entry
2 Shower
3 Storage
4 Garage

SECOND FLOOR

1 Living
2 Screen Porch
3 Kitchen
4 Bath
5 Bedroom

MEZZANINE

1 Bedroom
2 Bath
0 Open

LOFT

1 Master Bedroom
2 Master Bath
3 Dressing

2

Figure 4 *Major axis. By alignments of space, structure, and fenestration, spaces for various functions are overtly linked. Lofty, centralized living space rests below cross bracing, while progressively brighter spaces of screened porch and deck beckon beyond. The ultimate focus of the axis, the view itself, orients all the southerly spaces. Note the integrated lighting at the structural interface of column and cross bracing (right).*

Figure 5 *Living area, facing west. Spatial and functional subdivision is effected by structural articulation above, element orientation below (wood stove and sofas), and light levels (bright flanks, ambient center). Note the consistencies of structural members, wall, floor, and ceiling surfaces and the 45° geometries.*

6

7

Figure 6 *Kitchen-dining area. A spatial backwater, this area serves as in-fill to aid in defining the central living space. Note the bleached cedar wall and ceiling treatment and the division of flooring types at the threshold of the kitchen proper. Note also the low wall, providing a visual block to the disarray of food preparation while allowing spatial linkage. Note last how a potential black hole above the kitchen has become a light well, via the lofty insertion of skylights.*

Figure 7 *Stair. Meandering carpet amid endless planes of wood, the stair is at once a violator of the dense northerly side of the house and a revelatory link between its parts.*

Figure 8 *Master bedroom. Above the architectural din, a placid space is wrapped with windows. Note the lowered location of said windows to aid bed-bound exposure to the view.*

rooms and a barely contained southern living area, reinforces the consistent progression of openness along the axis between entry and release.

As a counterpoint to the ordered organization of space and structure, the stair meanders up through four levels of inhabitation—at times violating crystalline spaces, at times respecting inviolate elements of construction.

Without order, a small house loses coherence and the ability to elicit respect. Without whimsy, any building is simply a machine for living.

It is on this narrow path between stultifying regularity and chaotic articulation that Alfred DeVido created a delightful house. Reasoned and yet thoroughly rejuvenating, its proud ascendant form is made coherent by its unmistakable organization.

The power of shock for shock's sake is as hollow as the dull clarity of unquestioned tradition. It is easy to be extreme, and in this way it is easy to make a distorted small house. The essence of sophistication is the ability to recreate life without resorting to sensationalism. This small house, while devoid of the cheap thrill, is thrilling nonetheless.

8

Wrapped in Wood and Air

Two Idaho architects provide maximum energy efficiency while effecting a dramatic design for a home.

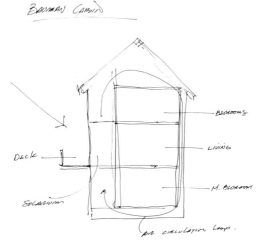

S teven Trout and Mark deReus were partners when Dr. Gerald Bauman approached them to design a rural retreat. DeReus took up the challenge, assisted by Trout. Subsequently the partnership dissolved amicably, with deReus heading for San Francisco and Trout building his own house near the site where the good doctor had his second home built. Consequently, Trout more or less helped Dr. Bauman implement deReus's design.

With the batons all duly passed about, the home is indeed the winner of this group effort. Its massing is extremely simple, while its internal engineering approaches the state of the art in energy efficiency. There are great pains taken in this design to gather heat from the sun, recycle it, and thoroughly insulate the heated parts to minimize loss. The house is of an envelope design; a continuous air plenum is created about the nongable walls and through the roof. The glazed southerly portion of this loop of space serves as an active solar collector, with the rest of the double-wall construction aiding in air distribution and providing insulating value.

The extraordinarily brutal Idaho temperature swings necessitated energy awareness in design, but much of this house is essentially a sophisticated machine assisting air flow to manage the internal microclimate. Aesthetically compliant to the technological overview, this house maintains its integrity as a house form, avoiding a protoscientific image. Part of the essence of both its efficiency and its successful blend of engineering and domestic aesthetics is its reduced size. The strenuous spatial demands of providing a convection space running the entire 30-foot length of the house while simultaneously minimizing the

volume of air to be treated required skillful resolution. If the house was simply intended to be an experimental machine for heating, then the architects' job would be cut and dried and this house would not be in this book. Instead the house had noble intentions of being a casually lovely abode despite the severe imposition of the air-moving mechanisms. These aesthetic intentions were realized only because clear-headed architects adapted engineering theory to human needs, to the site used for the house, and to their own personal views of the state of domestic aesthetics.

As mentioned, the two dominant means to addressing energy-efficient design in this house were the use of the overt air-management system of the continuous air plenum about the long direction of the house form and the conscientious attempt to limit the amount of air to be heated by reducing the size of the inhabitable house itself. The first effort could have been simply a technological tack-on, with a southerly greenhouse feeding heated air to a continuous interstitial space wrapping about the roof and north wall and through the basement. Instead, deReus opted to integrate the southerly convection space in form and use its dramatic verticality to embrace expressive elements of structure, internal deck, open stair, and hot tub. The exterior simplification to reduce both heat-radiating surface and air volume could have resulted in a stark, formal black box. But again the architect utilized an unheated garage to extend a shed roof and applied an extensive array of multi-level decks to enliven the exterior form, as it projects into a ravine. These decks also serve to expand the house functionally in the fair weather. Last, an applied shed roof over one corner of the deck

LIST OF PARTICULARS

Bauman cabin

Location: McCall, Idaho

Architects: Mark deReus assisted by Steven Trout

Budget: Not available

Nominal space: 2100 square feet

Perceived space: 2700 square feet

1

All photos by Steve Trout

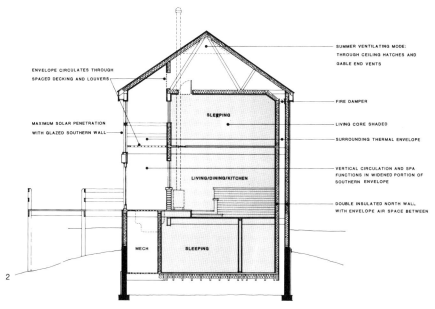

ENVELOPE CIRCULATES THROUGH
SPACED DECKING AND LOUVERS

MAXIMUM SOLAR PENETRATION
WITH GLAZED SOUTHERN WALL

SLEEPING

LIVING/DINING/KITCHEN

MECH   SLEEPING

SUMMER VENTILATING MODE:
THROUGH CEILING HATCHES AND
GABLE END VENTS

FIRE DAMPER

LIVING CORE SHADED

SURROUNDING THERMAL ENVELOPE

VERTICAL CIRCULATION AND SPA
FUNCTIONS IN WIDENED PORTION OF
SOUTHERN ENVELOPE

DOUBLE INSULATED NORTH WALL
WITH ENVELOPE AIR SPACE BETWEEN

2

All drawings by Mark deReus

Figure 1 *Entry, south. Perched on the edge of a dramatic drop, the house addresses the view with little apprehension. A simple gable form has a shed applied to its west side; the intersection of these two forms becomes the entry. The deck springs forth at this intersection as well. Note the thoroughly expressive, diagonal structural bracing seen through the transparent southerly skin (behind which sits the heat-generating end of the continuous air-circulation loop).*

Figure 2 *Solar section.*

Figure 3 *Southeast. A simple house form sits upon a steep grade, producing the opportunity for formal drama. Eave lines and deck edges are implicitly linked—through consistent sizing, finish, and treatment—as horizontal layering lines.*

Figure 4 *The convection wall. The major facade feature of the house is the thoroughly glazed southerly wall, allowing for maximum solar gain, while expressing the framing of the house structure.*

3

4

5

6

Figure 5 *The convection space. Facing east, the open wall of air is given scale by the imposition of deck and open stair. A painted gypsum-board ceiling adds contrast to the unending wooden detailing.*

Figure 6 *Convection space, facing west. A lofty space and expressed structure convey a grand scale and specific structural detailing. Note the open rails, stair risers, and diagonal bracing. Note, too, the custom steel brackets at all significant corner conditions of the framing.*

7

Figure 7 *Adequate counter and table space is effected by a tight galley organization, combining usable floor area with circulation space on a one-for-one basis. Both of these features are good examples of efficient planning. Note the open beaming and exposed floor deck underside above.*

Figure 8 *Living area. With thoroughly integrated seating, the occupancy per square foot is maximized. The potential for preceptual squeeze is eliminated by the open orientation out through full-width corner glazing. Spatial distinction from the adjacent kitchen-dining area is effected by a slight level change and a low wall divider.*

Figure 9 *Bedroom. Use of north-wall built-ins provides storage space to free up southern exposure and thus relieve the potential squeeze of a small bedroom.*

Figure 10 *Floor plans. The entry level is set to accept traffic at grade, while the drop-off facilitates an isolated master bedroom below (and space for a future playroom). Guests' beds are given an overlook posture above the basic house mass. The entry-level flow is given over to all public functions, with all wet and storage areas aligned to the blank north wall (which also contains the return-air plenum). Held distinct from these public spaces is the 7-foot southerly bay of double-height convection space that links the top two floors and provides access to the lower floor while accommodating an upper balcony and lower hot tub. The decks applied to the south and east sides provide spatial relief from the tight floor plan of the enclosed public areas.*

8

9

both mimics the garage in form and further extends the reduced house mass perceptually. The exterior surfaces are all natural materials, either lightly stained clapboards or unfinished cedar shingles left to weather. The eaves are broad, but the overhangs are not extraordinary, as the depth of the southerly convection space serves to screen out unwanted summer overheating.

The plan responds to these formal and technological limitations to both condense serving spaces for efficiency and to orient those spaces that should not be constricted—living room and bedrooms—to the fabulous views offered up by the hilltop site.

Structurally the house is a post-and-beam construction, allowing for exposed framing and open floor cavities. The ubiquitous exposed wood is thoroughly evocative of the classic cabin, made aesthetically rich by a flood of finished wood surfaces.

The kitchen is a tight galley with wraparound storage wall; the dining area is then nestled within the kitchen's dense arrangement of storage. The living area uses an integral seating arrangement to maximize the human accommodation per square foot. Baths are part of the narrow bay of opaque spaces oriented to the north wall (including the air-return space noted); the bedrooms themselves are separated from the entry-living floor into children's or guests' rooms above and master bedroom below. The upper-level bedrooms have an interior deck set in the large-scale convection space, while the lower-level bedroom launches its own distinct deck into the ravine.

The interior is laminated with pine, except for the ceilings, which are of painted gypsum board. Simple custom built-ins for storage (also of pine) create a sense of a thoroughly efficient, customized interior.

The single thoroughly uncompromised space in the house is the most energy-imperative—the double-height southerly convection hall. Its verticality, its glass-shrouded openness, and its expressively inserted elements evoke a powerful sense of space—powerful enough to allow the main body of the house to become subdominant without apparent compromise.

It is not enough to simply reduce the square footages applied to a house to create a reduced-size home. The effects of unconsidered constriction chafe our senses and bind our spirits to the point where livability becomes questionable.

The implications of creating an envelope house were drastic to the planning and massing of the Bauman cabin. Similarly the site had to be recognized. And last, if the volume of space was not fine-tuned to effect the maximum benefit of all the attention to technology, then the home would simply be an inefficient use of a great deal of creative thought.

Mark deReus, with Steven Trout's help, has not only solved the obvious problems of making this home habitable and functionally innovative, he has addressed the subtle problems of formal expression, spatial relief, and perceptual hierarchy. The results mesh science, art, and the human spirit with a quiet brilliance perfectly compatible with the beautiful wilds of Idaho.

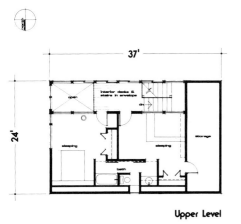

Upper Level

Main Level

Lower Level

10

Addressing the View

A summer house becomes fantastic via some careful craziness.

Summer houses by their nature are compact, utilitarian, and dominated internally and externally by the natural prospects that made their locations desirable in the first place.

When Graham Gund was asked to design a modest summer house in coastal Massachusetts, he found the requirements of the owners quite familiar: simply to accommodate a family of four and a wonderful view. Given the predictability of the program, an average architect might create a poignant, decorated shed of simple lines and broad glazing. But Graham Gund does not take opportunity lightly. Obviously the windswept peninsular site allowed sweeping vistas and yet called for low building mass. Exterior spaces had to be large and semisheltered, but bedrooms had to provide simple human accommodation only.

It is in the essential dialogue of public and private, both within and without the house, that Gund found his starting place for architectural innovation.

As said, public spaces facing dramatic vistas demand sufficient fenestration to display the view to the inhabitants and thus orient the house. However, cozy bedrooms have their intimacy compromised by unrestricted visual linkage to the outside world. Public and private spaces alike need to view the raison d'être for the house—the water it sits beside—but there are vast differences in the nature of the glazing used to facilitate the visual link.

Architects do their work well when they articulate differences while addressing the latent design criteria established by the owners and the building site. In an undesigned home, rooms with views simply get bigger windows. In a well-designed home, windows can express

themselves and enhance both the house and the view captured.

So it is with this house. The first floor, a public space, stakes out a rectilinear perimeter of deck edge and corresponding eave above, while the actual enclosing membrane is pulled back to define the identities of the internal spaces accommodated. With a membrane of consistent windows, the undulating wall, seemingly responding to the inflated air of the spaces enclosed, has a life of its own; it is a consistent system in counterpoint to and in concert with the other parts of the house.

In opposition to the window-as-wall system of the first-floor, view-oriented portion of the house, a window-as-object-frame system is executed on the second floor of bedrooms. Innovation is the extension of creativity beyond the barriers of expectation. Graham Gund has taken the concept of a simple dormer framing a view and cast it in a new, playful light.

Objectification of any building element is effected via several means. Primarily, the identity of an object can be expressed by the reduction of dissipating, competitive elements. The enhanced contrast of an element versus its context creates a focus impossible in standard detailing and construction.

As said, the meandering first-floor glazing wall exists in the horizontal confines of deck and eave. The consistent eave creates a simple roof profile, the perfect foil for expressive dormer fenestration. The nature of objectification is best served by inconsistent application of the objects set apart from their context. Gund essentially seized on centered shapes—square, circle, and diamond—made them windows, and formed the roof about their presence.

ARCHITECT'S STATEMENT

On the coast of Massachusetts, this sloped site, overgrown with dense scrub, lies within a summer colony populated by weathered shingled houses of modest, varied masses. This summer house for a family of four has modest bedrooms but larger-scaled open living spaces.

In order to take advantage of the views and the hillside site and to exploit impressions of summer life at the water's edge, the house becomes a large porch with enclosed and open-to-the-air spaces on three sides, protected by a hovering roof.

Dormers, punctuating the roof, vary the shape of the bedrooms within and provide specially created views at different levels for each space, including a skylit view from the top bunk in the children's room.

Graham Gund

LIST OF PARTICULARS

Davis house

Location: Mishaum Point, South Dartmouth, Massachusetts

Architect: Graham Gund

Budget: Not available

Nominal space: 2400 square feet

Perceived space: 2700 square feet

Figure 1 *Entry. Here we have a blank facade perforated by squared windows, porch-end voids, and the central entry. Ornament is abstracted as the unapologetic downspout and organic lattice help focus attention to the doorway. Note the proper paint and the absence of an overhang on this facade, in counterpoint to the natural-shingled roof and walls.*

Figure 2 *Addressing the view. Consistent eave lines and rooflines are counterpointed by projecting objectified dormers above and recessive, convoluted, meandering window wall below. Note the invisibility of the rooftop deck.*

1

All photos by Steve Rosenthal

2

3

4

5

Figure 3 *Deck and window wall. A consistent perimeter of eave, benches, deck edge, and columns is both perforated (above) and counterpointed by the living room (center) and dining room (right) pavilions. Between these two positive forms is the deck access.*

Figure 4 *Living room, axis. Consistent window heights and trim lines reinforce the continuity of the enclosing walls (right). This centered space has both exterior focus (water) and interior focus (hearth). The counterpoint to the space and centers is the distant dining area (center), both beckoning and distinct.*

Figure 5 *Dining room. Subdominant to the living area, this room is scaled to the table and addresses the view (left) and the kitchen (right), while the distant living room beyond presents a coy promise of future occupancy.*

Figure 6 *Stair. Shown with its hatch popped open, this major vertical axis provides a spatial counterpoint to the flat ceiling and eaves of the first floor. Note the integral bench (right) and the simplified ladder stair with open risers. The detailing of these pieces has the considered elegance of rational utility in counterpoint to the semi-weightless orbs at the newel points.*

6

Figure 7 *Bedroom. Beveling ceiling planes give way to objectified dormers, which are simply standard windows tightly framed by the dormer construction (note that the diamond dormer to the left is the same as the one to the right but rotated 45°). Note that the knee wall is oriented to the window plane and that the views framed are focused not only by the windows themselves but by their incised subspaces. Note also the lofty, subdominant skylight to the upper left.*

Figure 8 *Floor plans. These plans show two diametrically opposed philosophies separated by only a floor plane. The first floor allows rooms to become pavilions, centered forms as distinct parts, while the second floor presents the rooms as in-fill to defined exterior lines. The only consistency is found in the east wall, to the bottom of both plans, which is essentially a deep wall of storage, stair, and wet functions.*

7

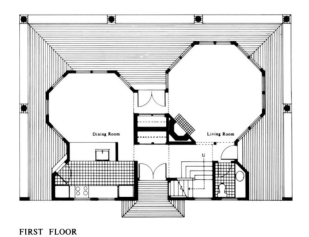

8

FIRST FLOOR

SECOND FLOOR

Drawings by the architect

The trick of this design is the formally simple step of incising these miniature gables into the roof planes as well as projecting their forms in the normal, proud manner of standard dormers.

The technological ramifications of incision into a roof, versus positive extension beyond its plane, are excruciating. Water enjoys insinuation into any concavity, and the formal voids created by incisions provide the opportunity for elastomeric membrane roofing to prove its mettle. The mettle of metal flashing is also sorely tested in this context. The aesthetic rewards for this care and expense are obvious, but the reader should know that there is seldom a free lunch when innovation impacts on the built form.

In addition to the animated window wall, evidencing interior spaces between the deck-eave sandwich, and the playful dormers, dotting a simple roof form, there is a third major building element contrasting with the form of this house. This is found on the east facade, or entry, the only facade without an opportunity for view.

Simply to wrap the window wall about the midsection would diffuse its impact upon entry. To wrap the roofscape around the house as a cap would ignore the orientation of the bedrooms toward the water, away from the entry. Instead, the entry facade is designed as a blank wall, dominated by painted clapboards. So whereas glass dominates one wall, and dormers the next, this third wall is simply a wall with perforations for windows and access and with an overtly decorative lattice (an organic irregularity applied to the wall's flatness). By recessing the entry under the second floor, beyond the plane of the wall, and by allowing the tree-shaped lattice to embrace the entry opening, Gund helped to mitigate the abrupt penetration of the house.

A fourth unseen element is supported by the three described. A roof deck–lookout is perched above all the articulations discussed. Invisible from the interior, this exterior space is a thoroughly experiential one, providing a gesture of pure surprise amid all the considered elements encountered. It also allows for the one thoroughly unencumbered view of Buzzard's Bay.

The tripartite exterior of entry wall, public first floor, and private second floor is marvelously reinforced by the internal planning. All service functions of bathrooms, kitchen, utility room, storage, and stair occur within the easterly, entry portion of the house.

A word on the entry: Normally, this book would praise axial entries orienting the entrant and providing a sweeping vista that defies the size limitations of the house. In this house, a solid core of storage and chimney opposes the entry—not unlike Colonial architecture—but the element of surprise is immediately revealed, as a vertical axis of space allows the stairway to be the major entry event. The visual lure of this element serves to entice those encountering the house into the octagonal living area and beyond to the columned porch. In this way, kitchen and bath are bypassed, and the sequence of the house is a roundabout process of encountering the unexpected. A house can defeat the constriction of its true size through spatial variety rather than through orientation of the various spaces about a common visual axis.

The second internal region consists of the separated areas of living and dining. The only horizontal axial linkage occurs between these two spaces defined by the window wall previously described. Wrapping about this public area is the consistent perimeter deck, edged in benches and columns. In short, where rooms aren't, the deck as a defined space is. Where the living and dining areas bulge forth, the deck is simply a walkway.

The second floor has the easterly service zone of baths and stair and the three bedrooms. Backed up to the generous stair space, the bedrooms address the views north, south, and west. The bedrooms are as regular as their dormers are whimsical.

A study in interacting identities, this house defeats its small size via the diversity of its formal and spatial elements. A variety of parts engenders delight and surprise when coordinated with consistent respect for the developed identities. Graham Gund has richly articulated this programmatically simple summer home to the point where its family of component parts fairly sings in multiple harmony. So much can be done with so little if creativity is given a long leash and guided by a clear head.

A Studied Starkness

Utilizing unexceptional media, Peter Forbes captures the imagination with some staged austerity in Seal Cove, Maine.

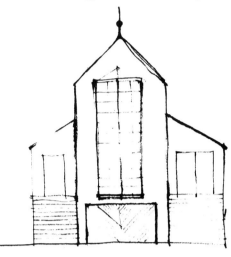

V acation homes are seldom luxurious, but they afford architects the luxury of designing for a greatly reduced spectrum of use and occupancy. The distillation of programmatic needs allows for great economies of construction. Generally speaking, when architects confront austere budgets and simple seasonal use patterns, the images of the projects that result are streamlined to the point of objectification.

Peter Forbes was challenged to build a 2500-square-foot house, accommodating three bedrooms, with the potential for a separate rental unit. There was also an existing foundation of an awkward outline already in place. On the plus side, occupancy initially would be seasonal and only a married couple would have to be accommodated. To add wishful thinking to all of this, the initial building budget was $55,000. It is barely possible to build a garage for $22 per square foot, let alone a functional house, even if it does have an existing foundation and a simple design program.

What is presented in these photographs is part symbolism, part spatial sculpture, and part boat shed, all combined to effect an innocently presented, but thoroughly considered, small house.

The photographs presented differ from the drawings shown because the house is in the slow process of being fully fleshed out in a finished form. If there is so little money, one might well ask, why hire an architect, whose fee is a total loss in terms of enclosure, heat, or utility?

It is precisely because this house had so many preconceived limitations of budget, foundation, spatial need, and programmatic evolution that an architect was *essential* to the success of the project. An architect sells time. No bricks, insulation,

ARCHITECT'S STATEMENT

The design for this house resolves a set of severe constraints with the advantages of a spectacular view and natural environment. The constraints include an existing foundation of difficult dimensions, a steeply sloping site, a restricted budget, and the owners' desire to have a house that can "expand" in the summer and "contract" in the winter.

The solution is a structurally simple building organized around a strong central axis leading toward the ocean. As you proceed along this axis from land toward sea, the building becomes progressively more transparent; windows in horizontal bands are more frequent, larger, and more closely spaced, accelerating toward the view. The axis culminates in a two-story-tall, triangular bay window commanding a 180° view of the cove and Blue Hill Bay.

Peter Forbes

LIST OF PARTICULARS

Wharton house

Location: Seal Cove, Maine

Architect: Peter Forbes

Budget: $55,000 (phase shown)

Nominal space: 2500 square feet

Perceived space: 2700 square feet

wiring, or fill come with the service rendered. However, good architects will earn their fees by spending their clients' money well, well enough to gain more amenity, utility, and efficiency than might be bought with budgets left untouched by architect fees.

The Wharton house is a perfect example of both master planning and clever detailing to compensate for limited funding.

Cheap materials usually gain a sense of tackiness when they are used simply to imitate more costly materials. Cheap materials also tend to be extrusions or laminations (aluminum siding, vinyl tile, asphalt shingles, textured plywood) artificially given surface relief or color to effect a result resembling a more expensive natural material (stone, slate, wood).

Peter Forbes has denied the status of interloper to these make-do materials and used them without aesthetic apologies or rationalizations. The skin of the house is Texture 1-11 plywood and asphalt shingles. The application makes these thoroughly predictable architectural clichés fresh and somewhat enigmatic.

The desirable qualities of both skin materials are similar. Cheap to purchase, quick to install, uniform in specification, and dimensionally stable, these skin treatments are not simply crude facsimiles but engineered alternatives. The awkward quality of their use is due to the often imitative nature of their application. Sheets of plywood, 4 × 8 foot, simply cannot duplicate vertical tongue-and-groove siding in any way save the most rudimentary visual qualities. Similarly, strips of asphalt serrated and colored to resemble separate pieces of cedar or slate are mere shadowy replications of the materials they supplant.

Figure 1 *The situation. Proudly addressing a rough-hewn cove, the house is sympathetic with the evergreen environs in shading and stature.*

Figure 2 *East. This is a thoroughly objectified profile, given scale only by the skier at lower right. Close inspection reveals window banding lines. Note the virtually nonexistent edge detailing.*

Figure 3 *West elevation. A flat profile of prosaic materials (save the central prow window) is presented. The power of the form is enhanced by its ornament-denuded skin stained uniformly dark. The asymmetry of the flanking shed parts is due to the perimeter of an existing foundation imposed on the architect. The axial organization of the central gable form overwhelms the dissonance of the saddlebags and is enhanced by window and door locations. The two-story window wedge is actually divided by the intersecting floor.*

1

All photos by Paul Ferrino

2

3

4   5

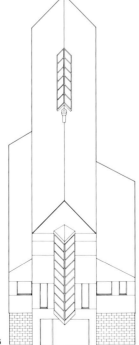

6

All drawings by the architect

Figure 4   *Facing west. Soon to be completely obscured by ensuing construction, this interior view displays the thoroughly mundane framing techniques. Exposed wiring, extruded flashing between plywood sheets, and raw surfaces stand in stark contrast to the incidental furnishings. Note the uncentered framing pattern on the gable end. The only thoroughly redefined element existent in the house is the large-scale prow window. Note the sheathed-over window framing to the upper left. Note also the unstressed tie rods tying the wall plates together.*

Figure 5   *Stairs. The single finished interior element, the stair splits to address each wing subbay. Dark paint aids in the ongoing counterpoint between raw enclosure and sophisticated internal elements.*

Figure 6   *Axonometric. Projected dead-on from the west, this drawing accurately depicts the axial order imposed on the existing foundation perimeter and the objectified exterior form.*

Figure 7   *Sectional perspective. A revealing portrait of the building's form, spaces, and structure, this section exposes the framing, which is impossible to see in insulated, heated, or finished construction. Vertical divisions from left to right are subdominant bedrooms, central vertical access, and master bedroom set above the major living-dining space. Note the custom skylight and divided prow window. Note also the tie rods in cathedral spaces center and right.*

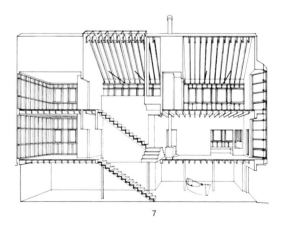

7

When used to create the image of historicist or stylized construction, these materials fail miserably to convey the depth of variety present in a less processed product. Industrially synthesized building materials are designed to be uniform and consistent, to resist decay or deterioration by the elements, and to appear almost monolithic. Hence these materials are absurdly uncomfortable—not unlike a baby in a polyester leisure suit—when used as an appliqué, stretched taut over a traditional form.

Peter Forbes saw this and detailed his skin to reinforce the latent qualities of flatness, regularity, and precision found in plywood siding and asphalt shingles. There are no moldings, no eaves, no eccentricities or gestures to another time. More obvious is that Forbes stained the plywood siding to have the same hue as his asphalt roof. The sense of an extruded house is thus presented, with dark-tinted glass fenestration set flush to the surface, reinforcing the sense of taut skin.

The very tautness of form, relatively seamless and thoroughly stark, helps defeat the awkward perimeter defined by the existing foundation. Essentially in the form of a lopsided T with a stubby top stroke, the outline presented no obvious axis or order except two abutted rectangles.

Forbes set out to divine an axis, extending the center line of the narrower "leg" through the stubby "head." Obviously, this left two asymmetrical wings. By formally relegating these one-story, shed roof wings to a subdominant position below the two-story extruded-gable form realized when the long axis is translated into a built form, Forbes created coherence from chaos. Part of this coherence is invoked by the articulation of an overt "head" and "face" for the building, addressing the cove view. Redirected spatial and functional focus has left the landlubber end of the house severely devoid of any expressiveness save a monolithic poignance.

Instead of effecting the sense of a lopsided basilica, Forbes injected the element of precise detailing of the exterior, allowing an aesthetic numbing of the surface materials described. The net result is a shadowy specter of formal hierarchy—a severe presence of axial dominance—overtly fronting the water view. The harsh potential is softened by the use of expressed regulating lines for window heights. By simply cutting all the siding to respect the banding window organization, Forbes used what most house designs bend over backward to avoid, the sense of panel construction. In the absence of any competing aesthetic influences, these considered consistencies wax poetic in their quiet order.

The severity of minimal material expression is heightened by the severity of its contrast to the interior spaces defined by the enveloping skin. The structural system used is as prosaic as the membrane materials described. Simple dimensional lumber of 2 X 4 inch stud walls, 2 X 10 inch floor joists, and 2 X 8 inch ceiling rafters, all 16 inches on center, is framed, using absolutely no innovative techniques. Tie rods are used to hold the walls together in the two second-story bedrooms that are cathedralized.

Despite the similar low-tech qualities of the materials and methods used to fabricate the shell, the exterior and interior are thoroughly dissimilar. The exterior skin is composed of sheet materials, stained or fabricated to obscure any natural texture. The interior structure is made of discrete component parts, their raw wooden texture left untreated, resulting in an exterior form starkly rendered and interior space busily contained. The charm of open framing is counterpointed by the thoroughly composed design of the shell.

The primitive qualities of the techniques and materials used can only be made poetic when set in contrast to the sophisticated specialty glazing of the skylight and prow window. The unsophisticated skin is given a dark luster via the quiet banding lines and shadowless detailing. Such are the products of an architect's time. The properties of aesthetic interplay described have no quantifiable good, save that they allow prosaic materials to have a vitality undreamed of in their normal application.

As this project evolves, gaining depth (and perhaps losing some incidental poignance), there will be one constant interplay. If there is one element to this house that is indeed splendid and thoroughly uncompromised, it is its siting amid the raw, brazen wilds of coastal Maine. This beauty was indeed the cause for any project being attempted at all. The site was the greatest challenge to Forbes, as its grand encounter to the water had to be well met.

By simplifying the form and techniques, Forbes allowed the programmatic requirements to be fundamentally enclosed. Without trim and interior finish treatments and without all the windows in place, this is indeed a "half-a-loaf" scenario.

But compromise is only in evidence as an ever-diminishing aspect of the ongoing construction. Peter Forbes has responded with a level of service rare in its thoughtfulness given the tools he had to employ. The unfettered power of form and space effected meets the challenge of an intensely powerful site head-on.

So much space contained with so little money and made meaningful by the dedicated application of a creative sensibility, this is a happy project that borders on the triumphant.

Complex Coalescence

A weekend home revels in the resolution of its colliding elements.

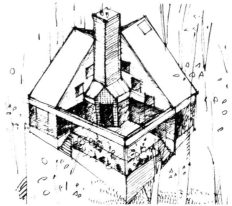

The ongoing game of small-house design is to create the believable illusion of size and spatial abundance. Architects can use a volatile mix of exaggerated scalar differentiation, they can situate the house to command respect, or they can provide enough variety of form and space to engender a sense of discovery and surprise.

Alfred DeVido has implemented all of the above in this complicated ensemble of various parts. It would be all too easy to assume that DeVido merely felt his aesthetic oats and went on a small architectural rampage against the mundane. But as a thoughtful and responsible professional, DeVido merely matched the intricate idiosyncrasies of his clients with a multiply expressive house form.

The parts as built respond to the needs Stuart and Deborah Minton listed in a thorough design program for a two-bedroom house with two individual suites plus a thoroughly detached office–guest house. As an advertising consultant, Stuart Minton needed the ability to take work home without potential interruption or loss of utility to his clients. Essentially, three full baths had to be created, individual access to three suites provided, and living, dining, cooking, and entertaining areas enclosed, all in under 2400 square feet of house.

ARCHITECT'S STATEMENT

A thoughtful, carefully written program was drafted by the clients calling for a two-bedroom house with a study, plus a detached office–guest house in which the owner could conduct his business by telephone when in residence.

The key ingredient in the organization of the plan was a request for a flower garden in the landscape of birch trees. Since wildlife is attracted to an can destroy cultivated gardens in the woods, the rooms of the house were planned around a raised terrace surrounded by a planter. Raising the level of the garden serves to discourage the entry of animals and brings the garden to eye level.

The living room and study flank the terrace, and a glazed dining room faces the garden at the intersection of these rooms.

Alfred DeVido

LIST OF PARTICULARS

Minton house
Location: Copake, New York
Architect: Alfred DeVido
Budget: $125,000
Nominal space: (both buildings):
  2340 square feet
Perceived space: 2800 square feet

The actual built form conveys the latent cross-purposes of a heavy functional load and limited building budget in a rather zesty manner.

There are five basic formal elements utilized by DeVido. Order was served by giving an unrelenting, bilaterally symmetrical organization to these elements. A short descriptive list of these parts follows:

1, 2. The two bedroom suites contained in the main house needed thorough functional separation; hence, they form two wings, with the first-floor elements of public living space organized under their definitive peninsular isolation. Access, common utility lines, and linkage to the first floor were provided by a simple collision of the two narrow, gable-roofed forms at a 90° angle.

3. The intersection of these two forms is mitigated by an overtly ornamental glazed dining area at the crux of the concave corner of intersection (entry to the house is achieved via a chamfered central entry opposite).

4. A large deck is created in the space defined between the two legs of the L, thus facilitating a square footprint on the site.

5. The guest house/study is a simple rectangular building oriented to the defining central axis.

Figure 1 *Various parts. Shed roof, glazed gazebo, objectified datum, and blank tower interact in a display of complexity uncommonly successful in small houses.*

2

Figure 2 *From the southwest. Consistent siding and glazing are combined in almost equal amounts to enliven this massive gable end. Note that the second wing is invisible from this angle. Note that the centered array (top) is in counterpoint to the window-as-grid pattern seen on the lower floor. Note also the vaulted interior spaces.*

Figure 3 *The ensemble. The main house (left) and the guest house–office (right) sit axially oriented, juxtaposed at a 45° angle to each other. Note the identical surface treatments and undisturbed ground cover.*

Figure 4 *West facade. Entry is revealed to be a negated corner at the point of gable collision (left); supports become remote and abstracted. The glazing patterns are used as centered objects for the bedroom (above) and as a developed grid (below). Note the shallow depth of the wing and the transparent relationship of the glazing of the wing end (right) to its opposite wall. By using inexpensive windows in coherently expressive ways, the architect maximizes their impact while limiting cost.*

5

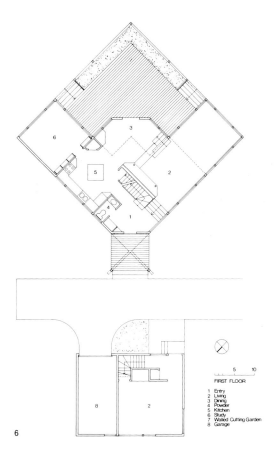

Figure 5 *Living-dining-kitchen crux. At the interior intersection of the two gable wings, a fireplace, level change, glazed space, and mixed surface media articulate the formal and functional interface. The exterior tongue and groove is effortlessly brought inside at the dining area, while the kitchen beyond has Sheetrock walls and laminate cabinets. Note the painted wood floor of the living area. Note also the floating corner mass above the dining table (the floor of the connecting corridor above) held in counterpoint to the glazed ceiling (upper right).*

Figure 6 *Plans. On the first floor, the classic layout of a bay between wings of a main house becomes a square when the deck serves as in-fill between the wings. The simple garage–office–guest house is centered on the diagonal axis of the main house. Note that the wing extremities are only 13 feet wide and the maximum span of 2 × 10s 16 inches on center. An interesting aspect of this plan is the asymmetrical positioning of spaces within a symmetrical layout. Six bays—study, kitchen, dining area, entry, and a two-bay living area—simply fill the perimeter defined by the layout. Although the second floor (facing page) is similarly "outside-in" in organization, each bedroom suite occupies one wing. Note the double-height areas over the entry and living room.*

5   10

FIRST FLOOR

1 Entry
2 Living
3 Dining
4 Powder
5 Kitchen
6 Study
7 Walled Cutting Garden
8 Garage

6

Five distinct elements, all in intimate intersection, could have been a disastrous aesthetic overload given the scale of this house, but several unrelenting consistencies have taken the confusion out of a complicated scheme. First, all the siding is identical in material and detailing—vertical tongue-and-groove pine. Second, all window detailing is similarly identical. All roof pitches, although juxtaposed, are identical. And last and most powerful, the over-arching symmetry alluded to creates a crystalline rationality where Byzantine confusion might have reigned.

The benefits of the formal complexity are manifold beyond the functional distinctions described. Two buildings provide a definitive entry court, facilitating a welcoming gesture impossible in a monolithic form. The double wings allow a virtual "outdoor room" to be created—rather than a simple spatial overflow. The counterpoint between the large-scale entry vista of tall walls and the occupancy vista of the human-scale deck and dining pavilion is made possible by the formal articulation described. The large scale of the entire ensemble does a marvelous job (when combined with a rakish site) of performing the magic of making a small house grand.

The interior of the house has only one axis, but via the use of a half-level change—lowering the living room—and the use of vaulted spaces under the gable roof, a variety of interior scales is created allowing the diversity of space to counteract the tight plan dimensions.

Although the complexities evidenced in the photographs presented caused large-scale organizational problems in the construction project (the architect had to become the project manager midway through construction and assert a far greater impact than he was ethically or legally obliged to do), the results are undeniable.

Aggressively challenging design programs often have blunted the spear of architects' design intentions. A muddied muddle of detail can sap the very aesthetic guts from any built project. In a small house such "Brownian motion" is the kiss of death—in either a functional, visual, or budgetary sense.

In this case, however, Al DeVido recognized the mesh of client need and formal complexity, and reduced the unnecessary elaborations upon the inherently convoluted aesthetics to create an intricate intimacy.

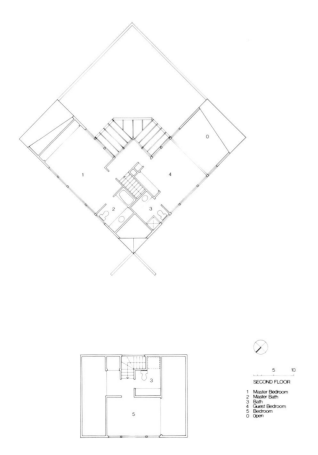

SECOND FLOOR

1 Master Bedroom
2 Master Bath
3 Bath
4 Guest Bedroom
5 Bedroom
0 Open

A Simple Complex

Fox and Fowle use juxtapositon to enliven a vacation house in rural Connecticut.

To accommodate ten people architecturally is an exercise in thoughtful planning. It is also extremely space-consumptive, as not only beds should be provided, but also the sense of space to facilitate comfort.

Obviously the easiest way to provide adequate space is to expand the house form to provide enough spatial lubricant to ease any and all potential congestion. The unabated agglomeration of space has been the norm for creating an easy house fit. Fortunately for the completeness of this book, Fox and Fowle were able to design a house that would normally approach "huge" in scale with a 3500-square-foot floor area.

Several factors helped the architects to design down the volume of space and effectively increase the perceived scale of the house. First and foremost, the clients provided an unfettered site, allowing a hillcrest situation rarely duplicated in an inland location. Second, although the building budget is not available for publication, the level of finish and articulation bespeak a healthy amount of money. Third, the built form evidences a thorough communication between the architects and the clients, conveying the needs of a young family with an obvious depth and sensitivity. Last, because this is a weekend home, there is a reduced level of occupancy that allows for spatial shortcuts.

There is an enormous difference between the words "authoritarian" and "authoritative." Given the power of the site, the expansive needs of the family housed, and the generous budget, a monolithic mastodon of a mansion might have resulted, creating an authoritarian impact on the site and family. The house that was built, however, displays the authoritative choice of spatial reduction

ARCHITECTS' STATEMENT

Situated on top of a hill on a piece of land that was once a cultivated field, the Ziegler vacation house has an open 360° view of the surrounding 80 acres of Connecticut farmland. The assemblage of three barnlike volumes, interconnected by a common entryway, is nestled into an intersection of eighteenth-century, tree-lined, rubble-stone walls. We designed the fenestration in the living-dining and master bedroom areas to maximize extensive views to the south and west and to permit passive solar gain in the winter. Sited among existing trees that shade openings in the summer, the Ziegler house takes advantage of prevailing southwest winds for natural ventilation.

Fox and Fowle Architects

LIST OF PARTICULARS

Ziegler house

Location: Goshen, Connecticut

Architects: Fox and Fowle Architects

Budget: Not available

Nominal space: 3500 square feet

Perceived space: 4500 square feet

implemented to *enhance* the net effect of the design.

Nineteenth-century mansions built by captains of industry often presented outrageously expansive billboard facades and unlimited site impact in the frenetic desire to display and implement newly harvested wealth. The result is that while awing the visitor, the buildings seldom seemed like homes. Often it was the level of craftsmanship—in the woodwork, detailing, or furnishings—that created user-friendly environments, despite the presence of so much out-of-scale mass and space.

Essentially, the Ziegler house represents the inverse of that paradigm. The interiors of this house are distilled in their detailing and simple in their furnishings. It is the diffused and yet highly composed massing that creates the sense of scale and embracing accommodation.

Essentially, Fox and Fowle created a three-part harmony of small buildings clustered about a common entry. In so doing, the architects had to guard against creating redundant spaces, as formal distinction tends to create spatial inefficiencies. Although the percentage of space given over to circulation is indeed high in relation to the balance of projects depicted in this book, the condensation of mass and enhancement of utility through a considered design create a very utilitarian home in the best sense of the word.

The various utilities of the component parts are as follows. From least to greatest in scale, the distinct parts are a garage with a storage loft, a dormitory building containing five bedrooms, and a public building containing kitchen, dining, and social spaces. The parts have several interlocking consistencies that preempt the potential for a discordant image.

1

Figure 1 *Site plan. Set on the crest of a gentle hill, this cluster of sympathetic forms beckons from afar. The arcing driveway creates a rotational prospect of the building ensemble, inviting encounter.*

Figure 2 *West. A duet of gable (left) and shed (right) punctuated by trees and underscored by continuous stone wall. Note glazed connector center and aligned eave heights. Note also the single curvilinear exterior piece—the fireplace ensemble (right).*

0 20 60

RESIDENCE IN GOSHEN,CT.
SITE PLAN

All drawings by the architects

2   All photos by Dan Cornish

3

Figure 3 *South. Bedrooms (left), public area (center), and garage (right) form a considered composition of distinct parts thoroughly integrated by materials, eave lines, roof pitch, and orthogonal orientation to each other. Note the existing continuous datum of stone wall in the foreground.*

Figure 4 *First floor. This floor has three rectangular plans, each set on the same orthogonal orientation. Garage (upper left), public space (right), and bedrooms (lower left) lightly pinwheel about the connecting glazed entry (center). Note that the cross-hatched decking helps enhance connection and axial relationships. Note also the orientation of the entire complex to the existing intersection of stone walls and mature trees.*

Figure 5 *Second floor. This three-part ensemble seems to rotate around a central roof deck. Note the cell-like children's bedrooms (left) in contrast to the open clerestory space above the living room (right).*

Figure 6 *(Page 171, top) Section through bedroom wing (facing east). The low exterior eave height translates into tight spaces on the second level. Note the bunkbed loft above the central corridor; the bed is set below a skylight to prevent a sense of constriction and to provide ventilation.*

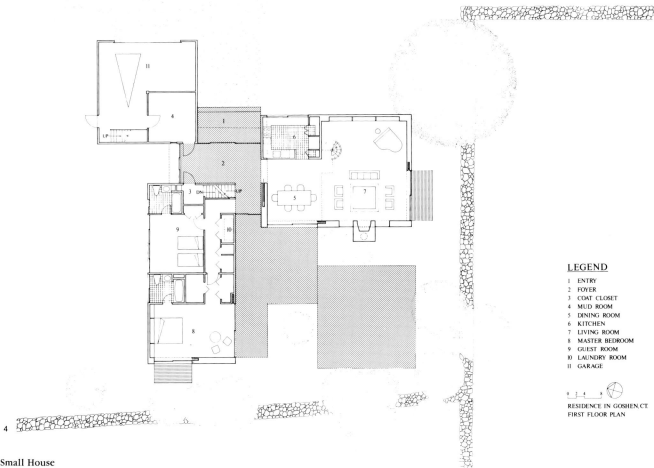

4

LEGEND

1 ENTRY
2 FOYER
3 COAT CLOSET
4 MUD ROOM
5 DINING ROOM
6 KITCHEN
7 LIVING ROOM
8 MASTER BEDROOM
9 GUEST ROOM
10 LAUNDRY ROOM
11 GARAGE

0 2 4   8

RESIDENCE IN GOSHEN, CT.
FIRST FLOOR PLAN

6

RESIDENCE IN GOSHEN, CT.
SECTION A

5

LEGEND

1   STORAGE
2   ROOF DECK
3   STUDIO
4   CHILDREN'S BEDROOM
5   CLOSET/DRESSING
6   RECREATION ROOM

RESIDENCE IN GOSHEN, CT.
SECOND FLOOR PLAN

Figure 7 *Living room. A vaulted space has its elements scaled to simplify their identities (ceiling, wall, glazing, and bookcases). Note the operable windows set into the triangular upper window for summer venting.*

Figure 8 *The fireplace. Facing west, the centering hearth, the single nonorthogonal element present in the house, presents both a void in the building's mass and the positive formal element of firebox. An insight into the thoroughly integrated detailing can be gained from this photograph. Note the integrated lighting at the beveled wall return at the roof-wall intersection; the wall has been thickened to enhance the sense of carved material, to house curtains (see left above sliding door), to contain structure in the form of box beams (above fireplace), and to provide a pocket for other sliding doors (not shown).*

7

8

The organizing orientation of all components respects an orthogonal grid. Linking all three buildings at their crucial near-juncture is a single-story, flat-roofed entry space (essentially the glazing in-fill space typical to modernist home additions). A series of decks extends beyond the confines of this linking space, finally spilling out to create a distinct subspace between the bedroom and public wings, facing the setting sun and shielded from the access road. On the second story, the rooftop of the glazed entry is revealed to be an exterior deck, linking the children's bedrooms to a loft overlooking the living room. Last, the materials and detailing for all three distinct buildings are from the same palette, creating a consistent diversity.

Internally, there is an emphasis on planned condensation of storage spaces and the creation of maximally utilized public areas. A bedroom has a dominant persona, as it were—sleep and clothing must be accommodated. However, storage spaces can be made more efficient by planning, and public spaces can be made to provide a sense of delight and embrace by their considered design.

Given that a garage is a garage is a garage and that the linking space is merely a blank connector, it is the bedroom building and the public building that evidence the principles of small-house design enabling their relative scale to be controlled and applied to create a rich ensemble.

The bedroom wing uses axial corridors to link bedrooms. Children's bedrooms occupy the second floor and have separate sleeping "cells" and dressing room/closets. The hallway provides three additional sleeping spaces by the use of its "roof" as an extruded bunk bed. The sense of precarious squeeze is avoided by orienting skylights above the aligned strip of sleeping space and leaving the roof uninterrupted around the corridor. The tiny sleeping rooms feed to a common room at one end and the linking second-story deck at the other. The use of pocket doors relieves these tight spaces from the imposition of door swings.

Below these three bedrooms, two suites of generous proportions occupy the entire first floor. The master bedroom possesses one entire end of the building and accesses two decks. With closets and baths as barrier spaces, the guest bedroom and master bedroom occupy thoroughly isolated postures, focusing away from the ensemble. It should be noted that a total of ten sleeping spaces and three baths are accommodated in 1800 square feet.

Contrasting with the thoroughly subdivided nature of the bedroom building, the public building is a large shell with a vertically subdividing loft, beneath which a combined kitchen and dining space is accommodated. The only overtly vertical space, the grand-scale living area responds both to the scale of the open countryside that surrounds it and to the needs of a family of five, plus guests.

The enclosing envelopes of these buildings are simplified to the point of barnlike starkness. Eave lines are low and aligned. The sense of richness is derived from the natural materials employed (cedar-shingle roof and vertical tongue-and-groove siding) and the considered repose of the complex.

As the house is set amid stone walls and mature trees, the farm imagery is not incidental to the aesthetic organization.

When diversity is allowed to express itself coherently, while engendering the sense of strength derived from the organized mix and integration of various parts, true architectural power is expressed without resorting to authoritarian massing.

The benefits of combining discrete parts to gain impact versus extruding their mass are best appreciated upon entry to the site. At the point of incidence to the site, the buildings are visually melded into a single complicated form. However, as the road curves to access the garage, the complex visually rotates to reveal the sweet spot of gable-end interface that is the entry to the home. Rather than the obvious force of a rigorously composed facade, this delightful surprise of an entry animates the encounter and beckons the visitor to experience the interface of these forms.

Fox and Fowle were meticulous in their design of this home. A large and involved set of construction documents allowed the fabrication of a thoroughly controlled ensemble. By examining each detail and prioritizing those that are passive and those that are expressive, the architects evidence the most appreciated aspect of their service: perspective.

Small houses are made livable when perspective allows the crucial elements to express themselves. In this project the massing and scale were conscientiously reduced to effect a sense of inviting informality. If the best of common sense and professional expertise are not applied, any building can grow out of control.

It is in the subtle invocation of complete control that this project gains enormous impact. In this way, the Ziegler house evidences the most sophisticated property of good design: restraint.

Attractive Subtraction

Addressing environmental issues with style, Richard Dattner creates a fully optioned, year-round second home on Long Island.

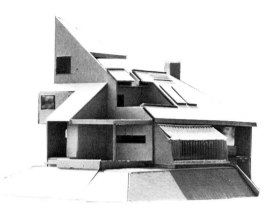

It is common for architects to use the device of applied parts to aggrandize their designs without breaking the bank. Richard Dattner is a New York City architect whose designs are anything but minimalist. And yet when it came time to design a second home for fellow city dwellers on a site out in Amagansett, Long Island, New York, architect Dattner found himself carving away large parts of his study models.

There is always ambiguity in good design: which elements of a building are positive, which negative; is space secondary to the enclosing structure or does it, in fact, create the need for the structure? So it is with this house of Dattner's design.

Essentially, the design began with two givens. The first is the wholly organic splendor of a lyric Long Island site. The second is the purely hypothetical abstraction of a cube applied by Dattner. As the site's impact began to mutate the pristine cube, the Cartesian ideal became a home.

Programmatically, 4½ bedrooms, a large living area, and several smaller subspaces had to be accommodated. Given the quantity of inhabitation and the site amenities to be dealt with, the resulting 3500-square-foot house has every right to be labeled "small."

The cubicle quality of city living engendered the desire on the part of the clients to deform the cubicle nature of the house as much as possible. The resulting house is a delightful combination of formal erosion, assertion, and addition, where there are parts removed, added, and sometimes simply alluded to.

Externally, a fabric of red cedar shingles covers all exposed surfaces that are not glazed. A proud greenhouse pushes forth at what appears to be the center of

---

ARCHITECT'S STATEMENT

The building form originated in a "cube" approximately 36 feet on each side. The large roof surfaces to the south and east were "carved" from this cube to maximize the area receiving solar radiation. The west walls are mostly solid, with a few small windows to minimize heat loss in the winter. The major views are to the north, so the windows on this facade are larger than usual for a solar house. Deep overhangs are provided on the east and south elevations to minimize summer heat gain while allowing penetration of sunlight in the wintertime. A second-floor, south-facing terrace also acts to trap heat from the sun.

Operable skylights provide natural lighting and summertime natural ventilation. Two solar-collector panels provide most of the domestic hot-water heating requirement. Two heating fireplaces provide additional heating on cold winter days. Quarry-tile floors in the south-facing rooms help to store the sun's heat on sunny winter days.

Richard Dattner

LIST OF PARTICULARS

Long Island house

Location: Amagansett, Long Island, New York

Architect: Richard Dattner

Budget: Not available

Nominal space: 3500 square feet

Perceived space: 4100 square feet

---

the south facade. Closer inspection reveals that Dattner has merely extended his eave line to the west and created a massive double-pitched roof lattice of exposed cedar lath, mimicing the shadow lines of the roof-shingle courses.

A double illusion is effected when it is further revealed that the north wall of this defined entry court is merely a pseudopod of built form; a narrow peninsular extension pushes forth the front door to form a distinct air lock beyond the essential house mass. Opposite the lattice and pseudopod-defined entry court, the true house mass has its south wall held back over 2 feet from the roof edge, allowing some shade protection against the summer sun.

Above the tripartite elevation of entry, greenhouse, and true house sits a double-hipped roof form that, not surprisingly, has its pleasant shape artfully carved to create not one but two decks, connected by an overtly sculptured spiral stair.

The combination of high-tech stair, greenhouse solar panels, and skylights is counterpointed rather dynamically by the natural siding and roofing and the somehow Shingle-Style-esque massing and geometries.

While the interior is fraught with dynamism, it has none of the lyric ambiguity between past, present, and future; it is indeed contemporary in spirit and detailing.

The aforementioned entry extension–cum–false front translates into a defining slot of space once it is internalized within the house form. The main axis for the house is encountered upon entry and serves to provide a rigorously reinforced division of space throughout the entry floor and the floor above. Cross axes link

Norman McGrath

1

Figure 1   *South. A formal and spatial potpourri,
this facade evokes a sense of kinetic ambiguity.
Positive extensions, excised voids, and applied
components reinforce and deny the perceived and
real forms encountered.*

2

Richard Dattner

3

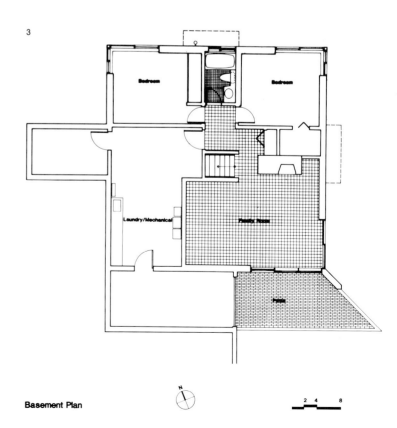

Bedroom		Bedroom

Laundry/Mechanical

Family Room

Patio

N

Basement Plan

2 4 8

Figure 2 *Entry. Eaves and roof planes extend to form a lofty lattice overhang. Entry (left) is simply an extended wing forming the back wall of the piazza thus defined. Above it all, two rooftop decks, connected by a freestanding spiral stair, reveal little and beckon shamelessly. Technological tackons of stair, greenhouse, flue, solar panels, and skylights are scattered about the passive shingled form.*

Figure 3 *Plans. Essentially, the house is a square plan with an entry-circulation slot that is extended to form a peninsular wall defining an entry court. The entry axis extends inside to order a host of elements, including stair, chimney, structure, and the north side of the major spatial hub of the house, the living area at the lower right of the first-floor plan. Note the cantilevered extension of the axis to the east. Bedrooms are essentially square in plan and are located at corner postures to gain optimal views and cross ventilation.*

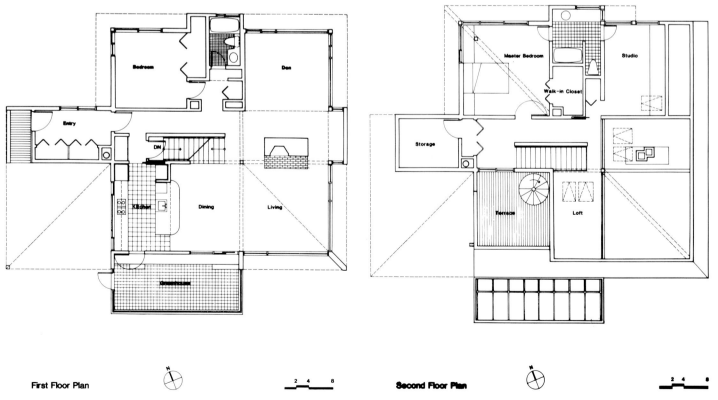

First Floor Plan   Second Floor Plan

Drawings by the architect

Norman McGrath

5

Richard Dattner

6

Figure 4 *Living room. This is the spatial heart and hub of the entire house, and its large scale allows stringy elements (wood structure and handrails), massive forms (chimney and stair), and obscured subspaces (den, dining area, and hall) to interact without aesthetic overload. Note the custom steel plates at framing intersections.*

Figure 5 *Master bedroom. Focused on the northerly prospect across Long Island Sound, this lofty perch stands close to the maximum height allowed under local codes. Note the column, which transfers the roof load directly through the cantilevered corner of the room, greatly simplifying the structural technology needed.*

Figure 6 *Axis. In its second-story form, the primary ordering axis aligns stair, chimney, skylights, posts and beams, and the human perception of the revealed spatial sequences.*

kitchen and dining areas to this slot of space and define the north side of the two-story living room at its terminus. Essentially the spatial hub for the entire house, the southeast corner living area is both a solar convection space and a focal linkage for virtually all the spaces in the house. A stair is inserted in the bold stroke of this entry slot, as are the chimney-fireplace, the skylights, and a major column-and-beam array.

This ordering axis controls a functionally large house and serves to increase its visual scale by providing sweeping visual integration of every major plan element on the first and second floors. The basement, or rather the "ground" floor, has a major informal family space below the living area and two northerly bedrooms, as well as the utility and storage spaces. The top floor contains the master bedroom suite and a spillover sleeping area on a balcony loft overlooking the living room.

This vertically stacked house provides a corner location for each bedroom. In fact, the very nature of a square plan tends to facilitate the corners being given over to distinct spaces, a motif carried throughout this house.

A secondary ordering element is the two-dimensional counterpart-generator of a cube, the square. A square is used as either an implicit or an explicit plan-generating device in each of seven exterior and interior spaces, not including the essentially square perimeter of the "true" house. Square spaces also define 45° diagonal lines, and when they are combined with the 45° hips present in a double-pitched roof, a tertiary ordering system is facilitated.

It is interesting to note that amid all the manipulations of form, space, and geometry, Dattner has eschewed the curvilinear in any save the most incidental of elements (counter corners and exterior stair). Given the fully loaded lexicon of horizontal, vertical, added, and subtracted elements and spaces, the architect has wisely opted to discreetly limit his palette to avoid dissonant overabundance.

It is in the hierarchical organization of large and small spaces, forms, and axes that this house breaks even its comfortable spatial limitations. The architect's insightful ability to know when to subdivide, when to link, when to reinforce, and when to remove emphasis makes this house a powerful piece of living architecture.

An interesting aside to all the competing elements of this house is the first bit of form manipulation, the truncation of the potentially pyramidal roof form to create an invisible sunny deck set at the maximum code-allowed height of 35 feet above the ground plane.

It is in the level of personalization of the house form that any size home can succeed or fail. Richard Dattner has successfully orchestrated an intense variety of elements with a single guiding purpose—to house a family. Without this essential hierarchical goal, domestic architecture loses all scale and becomes more polemical than personal.

4

Norman McGrath

RENDERED RESIDENCES

Either unfinished or unbuilt, these projects convey the essential tools employed by architects to effect the desired result of liberating small homes from the preconception that such projects are merely compromises.

I n truth, reduced size is an enabler of enhanced detail, invigorated image, and aesthetic innovation. These intangibles are often best conveyed in the architectural language of drawing. Rendered solutions tend to enhance latent symbolism and essential design intentions.

In this way, this section conveys the architectural shorthand that facilitates the creativity needed to defeat the spatial squeeze imposed on small houses.

Part art, part building, part unrestrained fantasy, these projects were all designed for real people, for real sites, by real architects.

In all candor, the realities evidenced are subject to interpretation beyond their essential realities. Drawings conceal as much as they reveal, and the images depicted are often more wishful thinking than nuts-and-bolts building.

All drawings in this section are by the architects.

Texas Town House

WILLIAM F. STERN, *Architect*

"The proposed house has been designed for a landscape architect. The client wished to reserve as much as possible of his small, 52 × 78 foot lot for his garden. The house itself is designed as a tower in that garden."

WILLIAM F. STERN

Balconies, awnings, and orientation to avoid the sun and enhance ventilation all conspire to make a tropical retreat deep in the heart of Texas (Houston, to be precise). A tower with a wing minimizes its footprint and provides maximum site space for a pool and garden. With acknowledged references to New Orleans, this house creates extraordinary spatial variety and formal impact because of Stern's skillful planning and sense of scale.

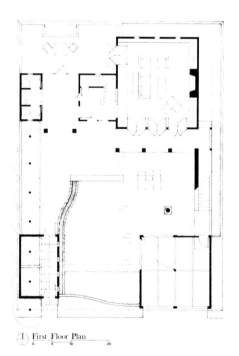

First Floor Plan

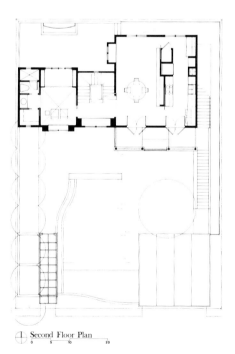

Second Floor Plan

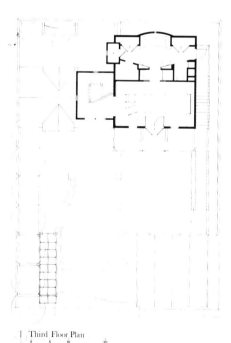

Third Floor Plan

Glazer House and Studio

MICHAEL GRAVES, *Architect*

"This small farm complex provides a summer and weekend retreat for a couple who spend the remainder of their time in the city. They have taken up farming, pottery, and painting as avocations. The buildings assume a rural, agrarian character and were designed to be built by local workers using vernacular techniques."

MICHEAL GRAVES

Designed as an array of small buildings, made large in apprehension by their detailing and juxtaposition, this complex has the dual functions of living accommodation and workplace. A domestic fireplace and exterior barbecue are monumentalized by Graves, as are column supports for an extended roof over the house. A colonnade-pergola connects the house with the double-studio building. Tiny and huge windows, extended roof forms, and axially oriented forms and spaces create a variety of elements that thoroughly defeats any sense of limits.

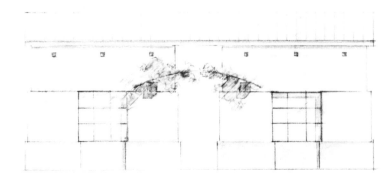

1 CARPORT
2 STUDIO
3 STORAGE
4 LIVING ROOM
5 KITCHEN
6 BARBECUE

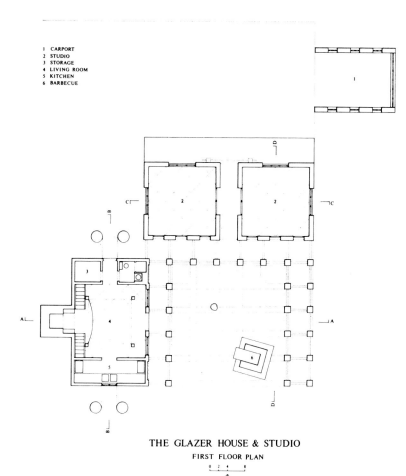

THE GLAZER HOUSE & STUDIO

FIRST FLOOR PLAN

0 2 4 8

N

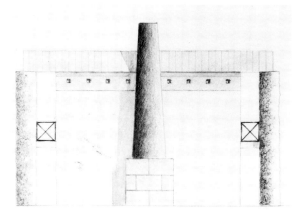

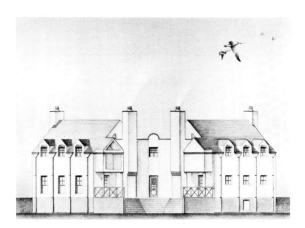

Copley House
STANLEY TIGERMAN, *Architect*

"The concept is based on E. S. Prior's "Butterfly Plan" project of 1897 at Exmouth, England. The site is a rugged, hilly, 20-acre parcel of land falling off toward a river. The program was to design residential accommodations for a single parent with an 11-year-old female child. The project was to be designed in such a way as to accommodate guests and formal daytime living requirements in an area separated from what was then to be construed as the private wing of the house. Finally, the house was to effectuate a 'civilized' facade. All of the above was to be accomplished in an area of approximately 2500 square feet."

STANLEY TIGERMAN

Three completely distinct bedroom suites are linked by their shared living spaced in two attached building forms—nearly identical replications of each other but functionally disparate. Axes, symmetry, and scalar manipulations are all employed by Tigerman to effect a "large" small home with an extraordinarily complex design program. Site orientations are directly related to the house entry and the building form. A study in connections and distinctions, this enigmatic mirror game evokes enormous ambiguities of scale as diagonal perceptions prevent an honest apprehension of the juxtaposed couplet.

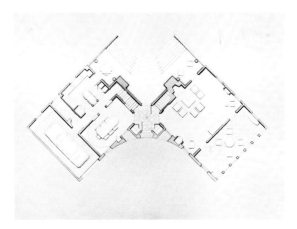

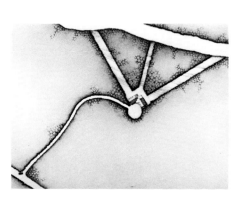

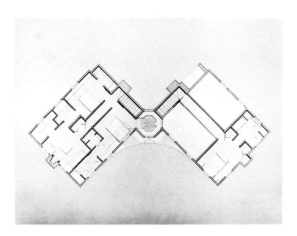

Competition House

SHOPE RENO WHARTON, *Architects*

"The house design utilizes the intimate imagery of a nineteenth-century American cottage without compromising the practical lifestyle of the twentieth-century family.

"This house is a series of contrasts that provides beauty and purpose to the different living spaces. It is formal without being formidable, interesting without being gimmicky, receptive but not malleable. The house strives to be a reflection of a culture rather than an industry."

BERNARD WHARTON

An extraordinarily sophisticated combination of rigorous planning, articulate ornament, and expressively simple massing is employed to effect a rich residence. A square plan extends to support an ornamented bonnet roof as each facade expresses multiple centers and thoroughly considered composition. The fully loaded aesthetics of this house implement a zestful embrace of all the latent potential present in small-house design.

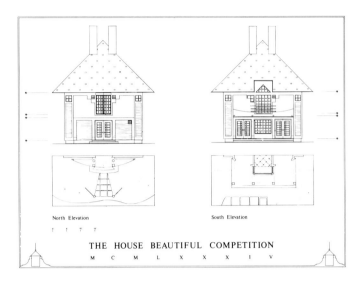

North Elevation

South Elevation

THE HOUSE BEAUTIFUL COMPETITION

M C M L X X X I V

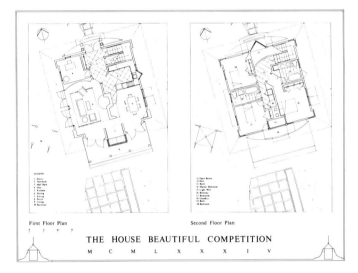

First Floor Plan

Second Floor Plan

THE HOUSE BEAUTIFUL COMPETITION

M C M L X X X I V

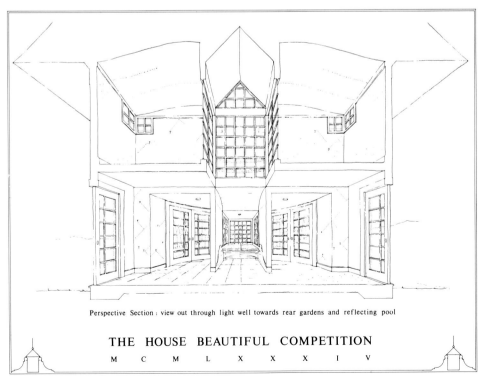

Perspective Section : view out through light well towards rear gardens and reflecting pool

THE HOUSE BEAUTIFUL COMPETITION

M C M L X X X I V

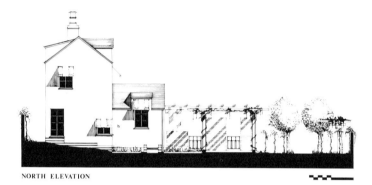

WEST ELEVATION

NORTH ELEVATION

Bailey House

FERNAU & HARTMAN, *Architects*

"The owners plan to retire in the house, have relatively modest spatial requirements, a limited budget, and a passion for growing things. They have divided their lives between urban and rural settings. The precedents and prototypes for our design are at once more urban and more rural than they are suburban.

"The result is an urban-suburban 'villa' that approaches the land with rural respect."

FERNAU & HARTMAN

This is an exquisitely extended house. A house form with extremely narrow bays, the form a simple extruded gable with an attached wing accommodating kitchen and back door. The footprint of the house is mirrored in the trellis layout. Axes and orientations create a thoroughly refreshing and yet tiny home. The house is at once wall, focus, and linkage.

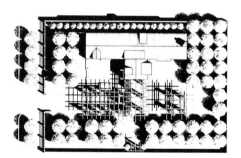

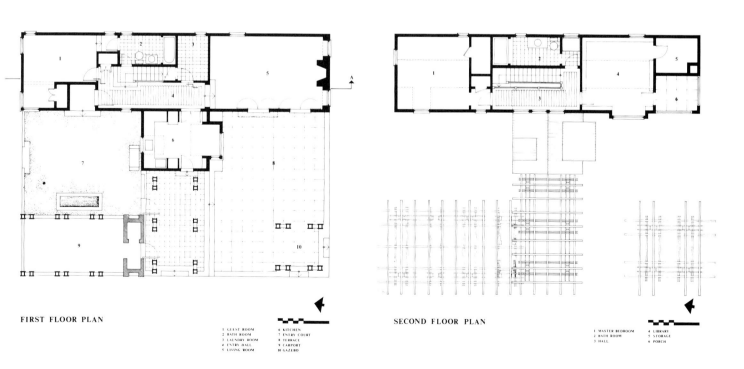

FIRST FLOOR PLAN

1 GUEST ROOM   6 KITCHEN
2 BATH ROOM   7 ENTRY COURT
3 LAUNDRY ROOM   8 TERRACE
4 ENTRY HALL   9 CARPORT
5 LIVING ROOM   10 GAZEBO

SECOND FLOOR PLAN

1 MASTER BEDROOM   4 LIBRARY
2 BATH ROOM   5 STORAGE
3 HALL   6 PORCH

MacAlpine House

J. WHITNEY HUBER, *Architect*

"The challenge of small-house design is to capture the personality and variety of living spaces more typically obtainable in larger homes. A little house need not be a little box.

"The MacAlpine house has a simple and straightforward plan made special by manipulation of proportion and scale, by control of views, and by dashes of humor and playfulness."

J. WHITNEY HUBER

This is a narrow-bay house that reverses the normal narrow-end-gable orientation to the broad face. Tiny dormers form faces, defy true scale, and provide formal variety. Roof extensions focus entry and create a small deck. This house has an overt passive solar orientation and utilizes its narrow form to provide effortless internal subdivision.

WEST   EAST

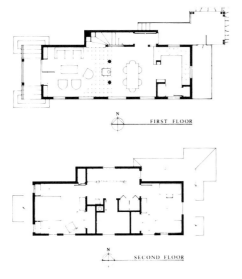

FIRST FLOOR

SECOND FLOOR

Proposed Residence for "Grant Wood" / Wolfeboro, N.H.   Robert Wagenseil Jones & Associates / Architects

Grant Wood House
In Homage to
"American Gothic"
ROBERT WAGENSEIL JONES, *Architect*

"The client, once having seen the flick Escape from New York, *did; later he inherited his family's farm, sold the main house, kept 25 acres looking over Lake Wentworth, and retained the architect with instructions to accommodate his current and hopefully permanent bachelorhood in a house that was to be, in effect, a freestanding, New York–type, duplex apartment . . . the shock of having left the sophistication of megalopolis being so great as to dissuade him from further adjustments to rural living in the form of purely horizontal accommodations."*

ROBERT WAGENSEIL JONES

A 1200-square-foot house is given life by some exaggerated down-home detailing. The simplest of house forms has a large deck applied to its south side and sits rakishly upon a steep slope. The slope, the deck, and some aggrandized eave detailing make the house charmingly eccentric. The interior volume has a single bedroom nestled above the north side of the house, freeing up the south to become a two-story solar convection space and spiritual hub for the home. Designed to be buildable in rustic environs, this home's humor and zest leave boredom behind in favor of a positive address of the light and view.

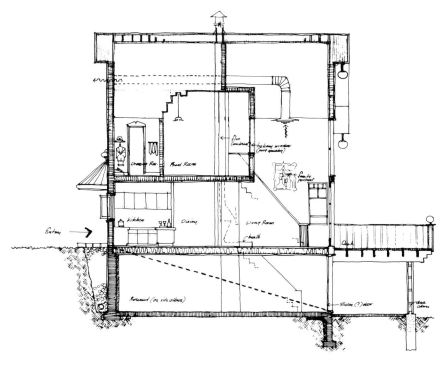

EPILOGUE AND RETROSPECTIVE

One man's art and architecture as applied to the small house over the past 30 years.

"It is hoped that my work will be an inspiration to architects and the continuity of beautiful inventive forms is realized. That the aesthetic exploration of all the facets of architecture, aided by the art and science of the day, will continue in making architecture the great mother art that it is.

"An architect must deal in the expressive geometrical forms and the way they coalesce toward the original idea of the plan. Always the plan is original with the creative architect. To the extent of his grasp of knowledge of the building sciences of his day so will be his success in bringing that plan to fruition. At times it may be necessary to create a whole new technology in order to achieve his dream!"

ARTHUR E. CARRARA

Arthur Carrara has practiced architecture for nearly 50 years. Carrara earned his B.A. in architecture from the University of Illinois and a two-year apprenticeship with John S. Van Bergen, an early follower of Frank Lloyd Wright. Having been influenced by Mr. Wright while studying architecture in high school, his practice was started under the influence of the master and the Chicago School. Since his apprenticeship, Arthur Carrara has been a life-long friend of the master's. His work grew to international exposure, and the focus of it is indeed varied, ranging from city planning to furniture design.

It is fitting that this book conclude its overview of small-house design with a retrospective of one man's impact on the genre. The following pages describe 3 decades of an examination of aesthetic principles. Many aspects of the projects presented are exploratory. Although all of the projects differ, there is indeed one constant: Carrara's relentless examination of the house as a tool for creative expression in architecture.

As with many of the projects in this book, that applied innovation was focused on those aspects of house design that both enhance efficiency and help reduce the size of a house, while mitigating the potential for constriction. In that effort Arthur Carrara has never left the cutting edge of architectural invention as a means to discover new forms.

Arthur Carrara's work is the best argument in this book for the value of perspective in design. As his work follows the in-progress works of the next generation of designers, it is hoped a continuity is realized. There are no pat answers in architecture. There is, however, the sense of aesthetic exploration that can only lead to the future relevance of the art and science of architecture.

All photos, art, and layouts are courtesy of Arthur E. Carrara.

Figure 1 *Living room, gable end. A standard greenhouse sits below an extended roof and between two concrete walls.*

R. J. Carrara House   1954
Whitewater Lake, Wisconsin

This 1000-square-foot vacation house evidences the power of clear expression. A prefabricated greenhouse has a floating roof set above its form with large steel gusset plates. A tertiary system of concrete walls allows the house to be set between two earth berms. On the interior, two compact bedrooms and an extremely efficient strip kitchen allow the living area to expand to a grand size relative to such a small house. The size of the living room is enhanced by the wall-defined terrace that extends directly out overlooking the lake. The Venturi Principle was used to heighten views and provide a "cooling effect", while the bermed foundation walls provide some measure of insulation.

Figure 2 *Interior view. A suspended fireplace hood becomes sculptural under the architect's touch.*

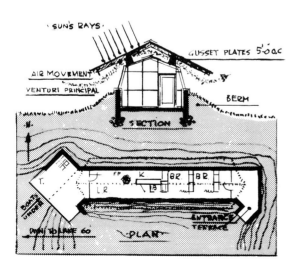

Figure 3 *Section and plan.*

Figure 4 *The house as seen from entry. Note the accommodated tree (center).*

Figure 1 *Living room. Note the custom fireplace and the square plan module scored into the floor.*

Figure 2 *South elevation.*

Figure 2 *Living room and kitchen.*

Figure 4 *Living room and deck.*

Figure 1 *Keel-wall end, showing the raised living area and the carport under. This is also the entrance to the house.*

Figure 3 *Entry and carport.*

Figure 5 *Deck.*

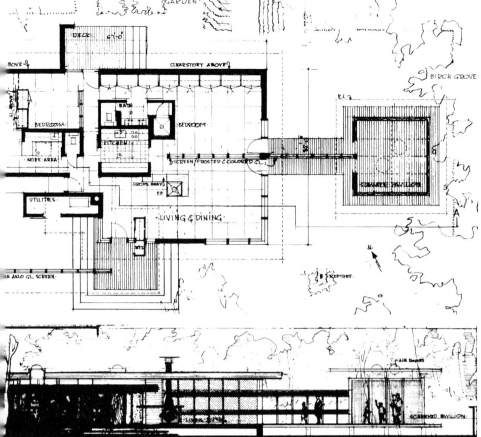

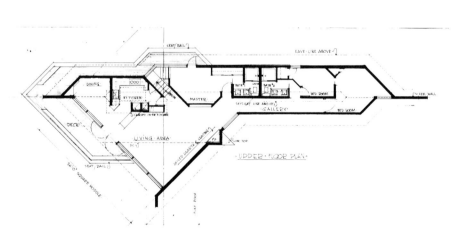

Figure 3 *Plan. Created by squares, the central square living room, bedroom, and plumbing core project several plan elements, extending the building's impact.*

Figure 4 *South elevation. With carport (left) and pavilion (right) extensions, a small house gains added impact.*

Hammond House   1956
Palos Park, Illinois

Designed on a 3-foot-square module, this 1800-square-foot, two-bedroom home uses a 30 × 30 foot central square as the basis for all the plane's permutations. A studio pavilion, covered motor court, and studio extension provide the articulations off the square. Extended roof and wall planes plus the remote connected summer pavilion help expand the perceived impact of the house. Set amid a cluster of fully mature trees, this linear construction provides a clear horizontal datum in complementary contrast to the natural surroundings. Internally a plumbing core serves two kitchens and a master bath. This arrangement acts as both a crux and an effective spatial delineator.

Figure 5 *Pavilion.*

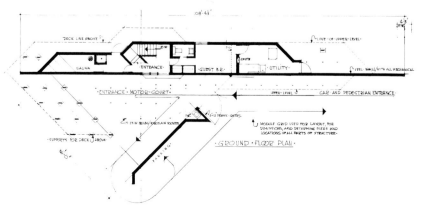

Figure 6 *Second floor (above) and ground floor (below). Entrance, stair, sauna bath, and bedrooms are held to one side of the attenuated keel-wall axis. The triangular living room expands on the opposite side of the major axis. Walls and roof planes extend well beyond the expected limitations of the building envelope.*

Voorhees House   1966
Colden, New York

An extraordinary home with an exquisite linearity, this 1400-square-foot vacation house contains four bedrooms and three baths. A 108-foot "keel wall" provides central structural support and utility access. The main living area is set one story above grade, with parking, guest bedroom, and entrance all relating to the expressed keel-wall element. Designed on a cross grid of squares set at 45° to each other, the plan evidences a sophisticated understanding of both tight planning and expressive spatial hierarchy. With wood used for most surface treatments, this rather nautical construction blends functional utility with a thoroughly expressive form.

Lasse House

Janesville, Wisconsin

1977

A composition involving a square plan and brick-and-block construction, this 1300-square-foot, 2-bedroom, 1½-bath house articulates several different systems. Lattice screens, linear skylights, glazed rear entry, masonry core, and hovering carport are thoroughly articulated and expressed. Wet functions are isolated along one wall, while bedrooms occupy another, allowing the living area to dominate half of the house plan. Closets, the central fireplace, and the aforementioned screens serve to subdivide the square plan's interior. Corner glazing and atrium skylights which are triple glazed are extremely important, both for daylighting *and* in the generation of the plan. All utilities are isolated into a double rounded form providing support for the carport roof.

Figure 4 *Door from living room. Note the extended cantilever at the roof and the seamless glazing.*

Figure 5 *Screen and skylights. Note how the linear skylights and wood screen are effectively controlled by the presence of the fireplace.*

Figure 6 *Construction. Standard brick and block used in expressive ways.*

Figure 1 *Central core. The fireplace serves as center for the linear skylights. Note how standard materials are brought to life by sensitive application.*

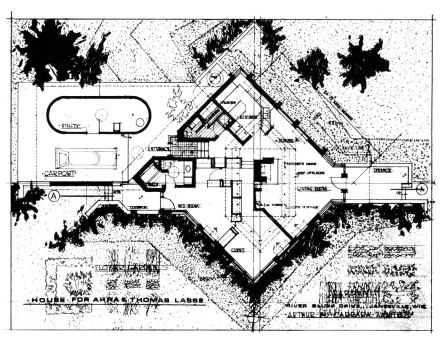

Figure 2 *Plan.*

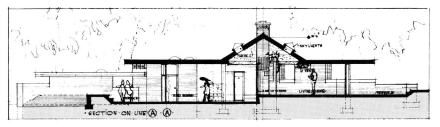

Figure 3 *Section.*

Clarkson Log House 1967

Adirondack Mountains, New York

A 1600-square-foot, year-round second home utilizes axes, wall, and roof extensions and cathedralized interior spaces to increase its perceived size. The log walls—"wing walls"—helped extend interior space in modern terms—but more important, it solved the difficult problems of scale in relation to mountains, tall trees, huge boulders, and lakes. Ten people can be accommodated in five compact bedrooms and a study. Because the sleeping accommodations and the kitchen are condensed, the living-dinning area can become a relatively expansive space. Increasing the fair-weather utility of the house, an extended screened porch focuses on a nearby lake. At the juncture between the house and the porch, a massive masonry fireplace serves as a formal hub to the interior of the house. All exposed materials are natural—from the massive stone plinth-foundation to the log walls and the exposed-wood interior walls.

Figure 1 *Porch view. Exposed and extended eaves, expressive masonry, and natural materials combine to effect a powerful image.*

Figure 2 *(a) Plan and (b) wall section. A simple rectangular plan extends its long walls and gable-end roof eaves to expand its presence. Note the screened porch. The section shows a simple wall construction of logs set upon a stone plinth.*

(a)

(b)

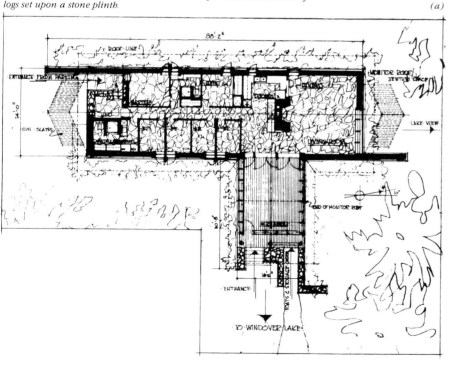

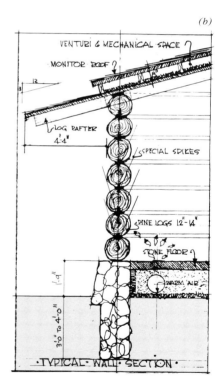

Figure 3 *Construction view.*   **Figure 4** *Masonry core.*   **Figure 5** *Wing wall.*

Architects' and Designers' Directory

Bentley/LaRosa/Salasky, 160 Fifth Avenue, Suite 702, New York, New York 10010

Turner Brooks, Box 2770, Starksboro, Vermont 05487

Arne Bystrom, 1617 Post Alley, Seattle, Washington 98101

Alex Camayd, Leung Hemmler Camayd, 305 Linden Street, Scranton, Pennsylvania 18503–1405

Arthur Carrara, Rt. 2 Townline Road, Whitewater, Wisconsin 53190

Daniel J. Cinelli, 440 Oakland Drive, Highland Park, Illinois 60093

Richard Dattner, Carnegie Hall Studios, New York, New York 10019

Mark DeReus, HDR Architects, 675 Davis Street, San Francisco, California 94111

Alfred DeVido, 699 Madison Avenue, New York, New York 10021

Duo Dickinson, Louis Mackall & Partner, 50 Maple Street, Branford, Connecticut 06405–8364

Fernau & Hartman Architects, 1555 La Vereda Road, Berkeley, California 94708

Roger Ferri, 261 West 22nd Street, New York, New York 10011

Peter Forbes, 124 Myrtle Street, Boston, Massachusetts 02114

Fox & Fowle Architects, 192 Lexington Avenue, New York, New York 10016

Michael Graves, 341 Nassau Street, Princeton, New Jersey 08540

Graham Gund, 12 Arrow Street, Cambridge, Massachusetts 02138

Roderic M. Hartung, 77 Main Street, Essex, Connecticut 06426

J. Whitney Huber, Centerbrook, Box 409, Essex, Connecticut 06426

Robert Jacklin, 182 Lake Louise Drive, S.W., Tacoma, Washington 98498

Jersey Devil, P.O. Box 145, Stockton, New Jersey 08559

William Lipsey, P.O. Box 3203, Aspen, Colorado 81612

Moore Ruble Yudell, 1640 19th Street, Santa Monica, California 90404

Thompson E. Penney, Lucas Stubbs Pascullis Powell & Penney Ltd., 255 East Bay Street, Charleston, South Carolina 29401

Mark Simon, Centerbrook, Box 409, Essex, Connecticut 06426

William F. Stern, 4902 Travis Street, Houston, Texas 77002

Stanley Tigerman and Margaret McCurry, 920 North Michigan Avenue, Chicago, Illinois 60611

Steven Trout, 512 West Bannock, P.O. Box 1552, Boise, Idaho 83701

Bernard Wharton, Shope Reno Wharton Associates, 18 West Putnam Avenue, Greenwich, Connecticut 06830

Index

Page numbers in *italic* indicate illustrations.

About the Author

Duo Dickinson, registered architect, is active in residential design and is the partner of Louis Mackall and Partner, Architects. He has headed or been part of a design team for over twenty houses in eight years. A graduate of Cornell University's College of Architecture, Dickinson has been published in *Architectural Record, House Beautiful, The New York Times,* and other periodicals. His book *Adding On: An Artful Guide to Affordable Residential Additions* (McGraw-Hill, 1985) has made a singular contribution to the field. Dickinson's own home, all of 1100 square feet, was awarded the distinction of being one of the *Architectural Record Houses* of 1985.